The Entrepreneur's Guide Series

ADVERTISING THAT WORKS

How To Create A Winning Advertising Program For Your Company

Robert Fearon

PROBUS PUBLISHING COMPANY
Chicago, Illinois

Library of Congress Cataloging-in-Publication Available

ISBN 1-55738-169-0

Printed in the United States of America

   BC

1   2   3   4   5   6   7   8   9   0

Acknowledgements

A few thank you's are very much in order:

To Gene DeWitt, President of DeWitt Media Inc., an independent media consulting service, for giving a hard look at what was said about media.

To Jerry Lukeman, CEO of ASI Market Research, who went over the research section and filled me in on ASI's findings as to the elements that do and do not help a television commercial to work harder.

To Lee Weinblatt, CEO of The Pretesting Company, who also reviewed the research references and provided his research statistics relating to the attention and comprehension of TV, radio, and print advertising.

To each I am most grateful.

And to Sabina Martin Milbank, Regina Davis-Tooley, Caitriona Kearns, Monica Ellis, and Antonia Carnevale—colleagues at The Creative Zone who supported my efforts with patience and hands-on help, a special affectionate thanks to each.

Additional Titles in
The Entrepreneur's Guide Series
Available from Probus Publishing

How to Sell Your Business for the Best Price (With the Least Worry!), Vaughn Cox

Entrepreneur's Guide to Capital, Revised Edition, Jennifer Lindsey

Forecasting Your Company's Sales and Profits (Quickly, Easily and Realistically!), Kenneth E. Marino

Cashflow, Credit and Collection: Over 100 Proven Techniques for Protecting and Strengthening Your Balance Sheet, Basil P. Mavrovitis

Funding Research & Development: How to Team Up with the Federal Government to Finance Your R & D, Patrick D. O'Hara

Initial Public Offerings: All You Need to Know About Taking A Company Public, David P. Sutton and M. William Benedetto

Mastering the Business Cycle: How to Keep Your Company on Track in Times of Economic Change, Albert N. Link

Forthcoming Titles

Negotiating a Bank Loan (You Can Live With!), Arthur G. Pulis III

How to Export: Everything You Need to Know to Get Started, Roger Fritz

Crafting the Perfect Name: The Art and Science of Naming a Company or Product, George Burroughs Blake and Nancy Blake-Bohné

Building a Winning Sales Team: How to Recruit, Train and Motivate the Best, Gini Graham Scott

Contents

Contents

Introduction

This is more than a guide to the basics of advertising. Its ultimate concern is that most elusive, ephemeral, subjective, and absolutely-must-have driving force of advertising that works—action-provoking creativity.

No action, no sales. Which is why it's astonishing that creativity is so piously and hypocritically exalted while so often being swept under the plush executive carpet in this era of global mega-agencies. Sharp-penciled financial managers have taken over the spiritual proctorship of these agglomerated advertising empires, and the concept-driven entrepreneurs who founded the premerger independent agencies and guided them to success have been forced into an institutional mold. The new leaders, the men of money, have neither understood nor been comfortable with the seemingly undisciplined, intuitive, mystical process of giving birth to highly creative, inspired advertising. What's happening today under their leadership is that the less talented, and the talented who will compromise, are forced to work on more and more accounts, pushing through first draft solutions, maximizing agency profits. In the process market impact is sought through irrelevant outrageousness, an approach we can label as pseudocreativity, propped up by heavier and heavier media exposure. Impact by the ton. The result is that action-provoking creativity, the fiery soul of advertising that works, has been elusive in this era of the simplistic attitude that if it's different it must be creative.

The goal of this book is to help you make sure that you recognize and get the action-provoking creative advertising that will work hard for your dollars, whatever it is that you sell and whatever the size of your company. To best do this it's most helpful to resonate on the same wavelength as those commissioned to do the creating. And that's just the reason why you should read through Section One before exploring creative processes in Section Two. Stirring up the mush in the right brain is tricky, and getting the left brain's house in order will be most helpful, if not absolutely essential.

At the end, once you've traveled through the Creative Zone, you will have a better-honed feeling for what makes for exceptional advertising. You will know how to recognize it and the people needed to deliver it, how to nurture it, and how to confidently manage the advertising process. You will be able to make better judgments on how provocative and creative (see box below) new advertising approaches may be.

What Is Action-Provoking Creativity?

Action-provoking creativity is not simply the outrageous, the ingeniously clever, the shocking, or the different for difference's sake. Action-provoking creativity means smart, right-on-the-money advertising. It's that effectively balanced combination of concept, positioning, words, photograph or illustration, typography, casting, editing, and so on that make a print ad or a commercial work. It is, when all is said and done, creativity that makes the things you want to happen happen. Unfortunately for too many advertisers, it is more the exception than the rule.

Don't expect a secret formula or even an infallible checklist of creative criteria. Action-provoking creativity can wear a million different faces. Which face you present to the world depends on a number of things—your company's corporate culture and marketing situation, how your competitors are presenting themselves, and yes, your personal prejudices and preferences. After all, one man's fish, particularly when it comes to entrepreneurs, is another man's poisson.

SECTION ONE
Some Left-Brain Nuts and Bolts

In this section we'll take a quick overview of the fundamentals of advertising, marketing, and sales and see how these areas overlap, interrelate, and support one another. We'll have a look at the ways you can get your advertising created—first by recounting the advantages of free-lancers; second by examining the process of going through your own in-house agency; and third, considering the needs of most companies, by rummaging through the tool chest of the advertising agency. With agencies, the better you understand how they go about their craft, the better you will be able to collaborate with them—and get that action-provoking creativity from them.

So read on.

1

Advertising Basics

I know half the money I spend on advertising is wasted. I just don't know which half.
—John Wanamaker

Be sure of it, advertising's fundamental mission is to put bigger numbers on your bottom line. Advertising helps do this by (1) creating an awareness of your product and (2) communicating as widely as possible those product qualities that you want to have known. In doing these things the desired result of an advertising program is, almost without exception, to provoke large groups of people to consider or at least begin to consider purchasing what is being offered. You have every right to expect that your advertising effort will move great numbers of people some way toward the sale.

Consider personal selling. It concentrates on one prospect at a time, and the purpose of the salesperson is to move that one prospect all the way to the sale. Advertising has a different mission than personal selling. It must precondition minds and open doors. It must support, not replace, the sales process. Of course, some specialized kinds of advertising, which we'll discuss later, are specifically designed to complete the sale or support an idea. Whatever the objective, you should not have unreasonable expectations of what advertising in isolation can accomplish. It works best, without any question, when it is intelligently integrated into a well-planned, well-structured marketing program.

Once you're ready to develop and support an advertising program, be very specific with your advertising agency (or your free-lancers or in-house agency group) about your expectations. You want advertising that is exceptionally effective in winning attention and in making its point—advertising that supports the sales process as forcefully as possible. Vigorously insist that your advertising be marked by creativity that helps sell the product. But realize that in insisting on exceptionally compelling advertising, you will then bear the burden of recognizing and accepting it when you get it.

One more important point. It is critical for you to make a commitment to consistent advertising that keeps the pressure on. No on-again, off-again efforts. Get behind that strong, creative idea, and support it with an adequate budget. Underbudgeted advertising, no matter how creative, is money down the drain. One of the fundamental characteristics of great advertising is boldness. Be bold in creative approach. And be bold in exposure.

Research that Proves the Value of Consistent Advertising

One telling confirmation of the economic consequences of shortsighted thinking and a lack of boldness when it comes to advertising is a research study by McGraw-Hill, publishers of *Business Week* and a number of other specialized business journals. McGraw-Hill conducted a running study of what happened to companies who did and did not continue advertising during recessions. The results were eye-opening. Those companies that maintained or increased their advertising budgets during a recession averaged significantly higher sales growth both during the recession period and for the three years following than the companies that cut their budgets. The advantage for the more aggressive advertisers was significant—and that advantage continued for each of the three years following the two-year recession period measured.

Likewise, a series of studies of six different recession periods analyzed jointly by the Association of Business Publishers and an agency specializing in business-to-business advertising indicated essentially the same thing: companies that maintained their advertising had higher sales and net profits in the recession years as well as in the two years following.

If you're really going to be bold, entrepreneurial bold, give some thought to this revolutionary suggestion. Consider your advertising a necessary capital expenditure, no less than plant and employees. Put it above the line. As a below-the-line item, it's essentiality is not as clearly established, and it's all too easy to have it be the first to go in a budget crunch. Cutting a hardworking advertising program is short-sighted and aggravates the injury, rather than being part of the cure. It is penny-wise and pound-foolish. Advertising is not just another expendable cost. It is a necessary investment for companies that want to stay healthy, or get healthy, and grow. Your advertising budget provides the seeds that will, with on-the-mark creativity, deliver a bumper crop.

The Many Faces of Advertising

If you're going to invest good money in this professedly recession-busting business tool, it is well to examine the nature and characteristics of this persuasive art. Advertising, as you've certainly noticed, is a whole lot more than Sadie Thompson in a red dress. It's everything from a 30-second television commercial during "Wheel of Fortune" to a single-engine plane flying low over a crowded beach, pulling a banner announcing "HAPPY HOUR/DRINKS $2/ AHAB'S TAVERN." It's a jingle on radio, a billboard along the main road to the shopping mall, a four-color magazine spread, an all-type stock offering on a newspaper's financial pages, an offer in the mail; it's even that offset, hand-lettered flier you've pulled out from under the wiper blade on your car's windshield. It's go, buy, do it now.

The average American consumer could possibly see or hear 1,500 advertising messages a day. The number that he or she actually does attend to even fleetingly, has been estimated to be over 300 a day. There is more than $110 billion worth of advertising a year, a dollar commitment that translates into roughly $1,500 worth of advertising for every single American household unit every single day of the year. All those TV and radio commercials, ads in newspapers and maga-zines, and posters, billboards, and neon signs help make up the over 1,500 arm-waving hey-look-at-me's day after day, 365 days a year.

In short, advertising is marketing's answer to the three-ring circus. Those who don't have their act together, who don't have the ringmaster or a barker directing the spotlight their way, are not going to sell many tickets to their show.

Let's take just a few moments to review the vehicles that carry advertising. Understanding the nature of each is essential as you consider the content and character of the advertising designed especially for a specific medium, and before you commit to spending any of that above-the-line budget.

Television Commercials

Television is advertising's featured act. Since the 1950s, TV advertising's first important decade, family viewing time has steadily been on the increase. What was a curious, adventurous handful watching an hour here and there is now an absorbed, unremitting multitude devoting an average of seven hours of cumulative family viewing time each and every day. The family that gazes together stays together. Just over 98 percent of America's more than 90 million households are reached through some 170 million sets. Each year there are more and more televisions—in the home, in the office, in limos, in public places. Each year more and more time is spent in front of those sets. If in addition to this you consider that a number of studies indicate that the American consumer considers television the most exciting, authoritative, and influential of all advertising mediums, then it's not hard to understand why over $25 billion a year is invested by advertisers in television in the U.S. market.

The 30-second commercial is TV's bread and butter. About 75 percent of all network commercials and about 85 percent of all non-network commercials are 30 seconds long. Those 30 seconds don't come cheap: television advertising can be very expensive, and of all advertising mediums television consistently requires the most substantial budgets. A 30-second national commercial during the 1990 Super Bowl, for example, cost an advertiser $800,000. (However, a 30-second local spot at 9:00 A.M. on a station in a city with a population of 500,000 might be only $250.) Realize that the negotiation skill of the person or persons entrusted to plan and buy time for you is critical. A clever, market-savvy negotiator can deliver a significantly higher percentage of the right audience for the same budget.

Some standard lengths for commercials are 10, 15, 20, 45, and 60 seconds. Some commercials, particularly for corporate advertisers, might run 90 seconds or two minutes. Others, selling goods or subscriptions offered through an 800 number, can run even longer. These longer commercials most often appear during non–prime time, when rates are cheaper.

There is another option. Depending on the product, the station's assessment of its salability, and the effectiveness of the commercial, a station might agree to payment on a PI (per inquiry) basis. These commercials, then, would ask for a response that can be measured, almost always through an 800 number. The station runs them with the agreement that they get paid a fixed amount for each and every inquiry that results. It can be feast or famine, but the station doesn't risk too much, because they just stop running those commercials that don't work. But if the commercial pulls in a truckload of orders, it repeats (and repeats), and everybody wins.

There are, too, those half-hour programs selling skin or hair treatments, real estate get-rich-quick schemes, weight loss programs, or anything else you could name that are literally half-hour sales pitches. Stations accept them as fully produced programming that will fill an early morning time slot, and charge a commercial fee as well, usually about the equivalent of four 30-second spots.

MTV, the Ultimate Commercial

Talk about half-hour programs that are nothing but sales pitches; what about those music videos! MTV's programming (and VH1's as well) is nothing but a series of product displays, complete with supers (on-screen captions) giving the name of the song, the group, the album, and the record company. It's the ultimate in sampling. One after another, all day, all night.

The cost of time isn't the whole story. More so than for advertising on any other medium, the production cost of finished material for a TV spot can be quite hefty. The average production cost of a commercial in 1989 was around $140,000, approximately the same as the national average cost of a single-family house. Some very elaborate productions go two, three, and even more times higher.

Not all is lost for the smaller advertiser who wants to grow but has a payroll to meet each Friday. A very simple, direct announcement can be put together for as little as a few hundred dollars. The rule of thumb is that the more the advertising budget, which generally depends on the more visibility the spot will get, the better the production values you can and should put into it. A lot depends on the product, the impact the competition is making, and what the creative idea is. It is possible to get attention with a simple visual and a brilliant copy line. Or you can do it with 30 dancers on the wing of an airplane flying through billowing cumulus clouds.

Just never forget that television is show business, giving us action, sound, and music right there in our very own living rooms. When it comes to advertising on TV, give a truly creative idea its due. The bigger the budget, the more important it is to do it right. And the smaller the budget, the more important it is to do it right. Strive for bold, action-provoking creativity, both for national prime time and for local, midmorning spots. Be sure to put into your commercial the production values that support the concept in the strongest way possible. And get adequate visibility so that all those good things about the commercial have the best chance to weave their magic.

Radio Commercials

Not only is radio in 99 percent of all households, but on average, there are just over five sets per home. It also reaches people on the move. 95 percent of all cars have a radio; that's some 130 million in all. And it's right there for nearly 20 million listeners even when they're jogging or walking. It reaches people at work: six out of ten adults listen to radio a little over half the time they're on the job. Put simply, radio may well be the single most accessible advertising medium of all. Now you hear it, now you do.

The formats of radio stations differ considerably, enough so that very specific audiences are attracted to specifically formatted stations. (But remember, when considering the creative approach of a commercial, that on many stations the audience changes texture depending on the time of day or the special programming feature.) There's news and weather, and traffic reports and business reports. Classical music, hard rock, soft rock, easy listening, country and western, and jazz are all represented. There are talk shows, call-in shows, dramas, comedies, and farm shows, religious shows, and educational shows. Most of the above can be heard in the large cities, and much of the above everywhere else. Whether the market is upscale and well heeled or pre-teen or high school age, you can pinpoint it quite accurately with radio. Radio is excellent for precise, local marketing.

The standard length for a radio commercial is 60 seconds. Shorter units, particularly 30 seconds and 15 seconds, are becoming more common. But without the visual element of television, the shorter commercials have the formidable task of registering their message solely by sound in haiku-like fashion. On the other hand, as in television, some products and subscriptions are sold on radio through longer-length commercials.

Both television and radio use billboards ("Be sure to tune in tonight at 6:00 P.M., when Granny Smith Computers brings you the news.") and sponsor identification spots ("The following program is sponsored by Koca Kola Hair Dyes. It's the unreal thing!") to support the advertising effort of sponsored shows.

As for costs, rates vary depending on the size of the market, the makeup of the audience, the time of day or night the spots will be on, and other specifics. What the market will bear and how good a negotiator you have are critical factors. The size of cost differences is indicated by the fact that while you could get a schedule of 10 prime spots a week on a major radio station in one of the big three markets (New York, Los Angeles, and Chicago) for something between $3,000 and $7,000, in Peoria you might get a similar schedule for around $350. PIs (with the advertiser paying per inquiry, as noted in the television section) are available on radio also. Specifying when you want to be aired costs more than if you let the station rotate your spots at times when there isn't much advertiser activity. There won't be as much listener activity then, either, but if the station throws in a whole lot of spots as a bonus, you could do very well. It all depends on how many spots and when they're aired. Working out the TRPs (target rating points) to your best advantage is a tricky business.

The production costs for radio commercials are considerably less than the costs for making television commercials. In fact, nearly 20 percent of all commercials on radio are scripts provided by the advertiser and read live by the on-air announcer or personality. For these there are no production costs, although sometimes you may have to pay a fee to the station announcer for reading it. For those commercials that are elaborately produced, with actors, music, sound effects—the works—their costs on average are somewhere between $10,000 and $20,000. Using well-known personalities, be it for radio, television, or print, will throw the numbers all out of joint. Some very hot celebrities have been known to sign one-year, exclusive contracts for over a million dollars. If you go that creative route, your spokesperson will have to do a lot better than Willy Loman.

One thing radio advertisers do have going for them, which leaves a little room for error, is that the cost per thousand people reached is lower for spot radio than it is for virtually every other advertising medium. It's usually lower—but not always—than television, magazines, newspapers, outdoor advertising, and direct mail.

Magazine Ads

The Old and New Testaments, the Rosetta Stone, the Dead Sea Scrolls, ancient Chinese manuscripts, the Book of Kells have all presented written persuasions that transcend the centuries. Today's magazine ads may not have quite the same life span or importance as these examples, but they have a tactility, a special authority, and a staying power that broadcast ads don't have. Readers can go over the message again and again. They can linger on an argument, look carefully at a picture, and even cut out a coupon or rip out the whole ad itself. Advertising in print is advertising you can pick up and touch.

All told there are more than two thousand different consumer magazines and a myriad of specialized magazines. These latter publications are directed to beekeepers, computer hackers, chemical engineers, soccer buffs, nudists, funeral directors, soap opera fans— all sorts of people with very specific and often esoteric interests. Each year, in fact, somewhere around two thousand new magazines are launched. As a result, over the last decade, what with new titles and more readers for the old standbys, magazine circulation has grown faster than the U.S. population itself—31 percent versus 17 percent.

Who's doing all this reading? Nearly everyone. 94 percent of U.S. adults read an average of almost 10 different magazines a month. It may not come as a surprise that magazine reading is heaviest among the college educated and those with household incomes of $50,000 and over and for the entire magazine-reading audience, most magazine reading—62 percent—is done in the home. You can narrowly pinpoint a market through specialized magazines, or you can take a broader, more diversified bite of potential customers through one of the mass-audience magazines. Remember, audience and circulation are two different things. Each copy of a magazine is read, on average, by three to four people. These multiple readers for any copy of any given magazine can translate into some hefty audience numbers. For example, the *Reader's Digest,* which has a circulation of about 17 million, the largest in the U.S., actually has some 50 million readers each month.

The creative possibilities of magazine ads are, considering that there are no moving pictures or sound, quite broad. There are spreads, multiple-page sections, full pages, and a variety of fractional sizes; four colors, two colors, and black and white, pop-ups, 3-D illustrations, scratch-and-sniff samples, and bound-in samples. Each offers different creative opportunities. So do inside front cover gatefolds, back covers, and series of consecutive pages. And with magazines, more practically and precisely than with TV, you can alter a specific ad to appeal to the specialized audiences of different magazine groups.

Newspaper Ads

When it comes to advertising dollars, newspapers are the big winners. The groups of 17,000 or so daily newspapers and 8,000 or so Sunday newspapers each reach over 110 million people, nearly two-thirds of the adult population of the United States. With advertisers investing a whopping $30 billion a year in the pages of these newspapers, that comes to five billion to six billion dollars more than the total annual investment in television.

In general newspaper readers are an able-to-buy market. Depending on the paper, the market it serves, and the character of its editorial appeal, the audience of a paper can be upscale or a cross section of the local population in its area. Looking at the national picture, a little better than three-quarters of all U.S. adults with a household income over $60,000, read a newspaper each day.

One of the principal characteristics of newspaper advertising is that much of it is geared to generating immediate action. Food stores, clothing stores, automobile dealerships, and a host of other retail stores live by newspaper advertising. For the great majority of retailers, television may be too expensive, magazines may not be local enough and lack the day-to-day immediacy, and radio, although a viable option, may not fit if there is a need for details or a need to show the product.

Naturally, a newspaper will happily sell you a full page or more in any issue. But with newspapers' large format, there are the options of a variety of ad sizes, down to a fraction-of-an-inch personal. Rates differ depending on frequency, number of lines you contract for, and whether it's a retail ad or a general ad.

There are also creative options to encourage advertisers. It used to be black-and-white and read all over; now it's the rainbow. The great majority of newspapers offer color advertising. Color in a newspaper means either two or three colors. With three colors you can achieve a good approximation of a four-color photo: certainly not the quality of a magazine full-color page, but really quite good. The smallest color unit is usually a quarter page, and you could reach around half the newspaper audience in the United States by picking out those newspapers offering color in the quarter-page size. When it comes to a full page in color, you could reach 85 percent to 90 percent of the total U.S. newspaper audience.

Of course, there are always FSIs (freestanding inserts), brochures or single pages that you create, print up, and deliver to the newspaper to be folded into the paper itself. An FSI gives you creative options from a four-color booklet printed on heavy, coated stock to a simple leaflet in one color on plain paper stock.

In general, newspapers offer the advantage of being a significant and vital voice of a local market. However, there are now some successful national newspapers. *USA Today*, the *Christian Science Monitor*, and the *Wall Street Journal* are just three.

As with any medium creativity in newspaper advertising can make a big difference. An analysis of readership scores for the same size ads in the same product category showed that the difference in effectiveness varied by ratios of up to two to one. Creativity that provokes action is not a luxury—it's an absolute necessity.

The Bottom Line

Why advertise? Because it will help you make a buck. Maybe even a million of them. Consider these points:

- Advertising that works can provoke immediate sales action.
- Advertising that works will keep your company as a whole, or one or more of your products, uppermost in customers' minds.
- Advertising that works will help keep your present customers sold and feeling smart about having chosen your product.
- Advertising that works will get your potential customers thinking favorably about your company and its products.
- Advertising that works can communicate very specific information in its role as "paid public relations." It can ensure that what you want known is presented exactly the way you want to present it, when you want to present it.
- Advertising that works will help build and maintain esprit de corps among your sales staff and other employees.

What advertising can't do is make a bad product good. Nor can it set an inefficient sales and marketing structure right.

But when you consider all the things that advertising can do, remember that it will do them a lot more effectively when it is constructed on a solid structure of on-the-mark, sizzling creativity.

2

The Marketing-Advertising Connection

One-third of the people in the United States promote
while the other two-thirds provide.
—Will Rogers

Winning advertising begins with a sound marketing strategy. And as you are well aware, in preparing a marketing strategy a precise measurement of the characteristics of and influences on the target market is essential. You've got to know, not guess. You've got to understand buyer behavior and motivation: what they want and what they could want. You've got to be clear on what function the product serves, who can use it, what alternatives (i.e., competitive products and prices) potential users can choose from, the nature of these alternatives, and how they are being presented. This, without a lot of complicating flummery, is essentially the basic marketing grist necessary to achieve sizzling, focused creativity.

Advertising itself must take an advocacy role in the process. Its most basic and obvious function is to sell. It is the peddler with his cart, singing out, "Cockles and mussels, alive, alive, ooh!" Sizzling creativity built on a sound marketing base is usually simple and right on the money. Years ago a country café along a road in upstate New York used to put out a sign, a large, neatly painted board propped up on a chair, that read, "Hungry? Eat here." Brief and right to the heart of the matter. Problem, solution. It deserved a Clio, an Andy, and a One Show Award. Not all advertising has to be that pithy and direct, but

19

considering the nature of that specific business, its cultural character and location, and the likelihood that a portion of the passing market would be hungry and therefore prime candidates for response, it was a superb creative solution.

The best advertising comes out of a thorough understanding of a business's customers and all the many factors affecting the sales process. It's your responsibility as the advertiser to be certain that the advertising agency has thoroughly done its homework and has an accurate understanding of the marketing structure in place for the product. Acting in concert with this marketing structure, the agency must ultimately be responsible for advertising that pushes all the right psychological buttons and helps sell the product. That's what action-provoking creativity is all about.

CAUTION:

Marketing has become a much-abused word. Too often it is invoked as a mystical incantation to suggest a sophisticated awareness of your product positioning and sales situation. Much advertising that has been constructed and approved as being marketing based falls short of effectively reaching the right people with the right message in the right way at the right time. Identifying the word *marketing* with the raison d'être of a creative approach does not, of course, guarantee that a particular advertising program is based on a carefully construct-ed, intelligently thought through, meticulously documented marketing foundation. Look beyond the reassuring use of the word in a presentation to the facts, the reasoning, the strategies that grow out of the realities of the marketplace.

This brings us to the clarion call for advertising that will "knock their socks off." The first thing to understand is that such advertising's principal feature, as intended by the one enthusiastically calling for such podiatric violence, is shock for the sake of attention. All well and good, but advertising that does not successfully persuade a significant portion of the target market to do something, buy something, or think something is a waste of money. Always remember that the fundamental measure of the provocativeness of the creative approach is how well it persuades, not how outrageous or different it is. Understand this, and you're well on your way into the Creative Zone. But be aware that evaluating the persuasiveness and effectiveness of an advertising approach is life on a slippery slope. What lies ahead is designed to help you get a better grip on it.

Marketing, Uncomplicated

Remember the five little pigs? The first one, you'll recall, went to market. Let us, for the purposes of this book and in quest of especially effective advertising, agree on what we mean by a *market* and, by extension, *marketing.*

A market, historically, is a place where things are sold. Marketing, *market* with an *ing,* is the whole process involved in putting something up for sale. A seller has a product he or she has grown or manufactured, or represents. It is made available to a potential buyer in a place where it can be purchased. The seller may structure a persuasion that works at that moment, or, with advance planning, he or she may have initiated some persuasions on the potential buyer prior to the buying moment; or both.

Whether at the point of sale, or in advance at a place where contact can be made with the potential customer, intelligent, creatively constructed advertising can critically and vitally assist the sales process. Advertising, please remember, must vigorously relate to both the total marketing structure and to the sales operation.

Actually, sales is almost always looked upon as part of the marketing process. But I'm convinced that there is an advantage to looking at each as separate, if overlapping, functions. Marketing is, in the best of all worlds, concerned with the needs and desires of the customer. Sales is more concerned with the direct act of generating income and, as a result, profit for a company. By so distinguishing the two, it is easier to understand—and this is very important when striving for especially creative advertising—that advertising functions best when its purpose is clearly identified with the latter (generating income and profit) while its content and techniques are concerned with the former (the needs and desires of the customer).

Advertising, Uncomplicated

A case can be made that the world's oldest profession is advertising, not you-know-what. It all began some time after pithecanthropus climbed out of the trees and started getting around on the hunt upright. Think about it. All those animals scrawled on the walls of caves in Lascaux, Altamira, and Niaux are really ads, posters, icons currying favor with the spirits who provide food and the warmth and protection of fur. The more animals successfully felled by a semierect man in the hunt, the more meat and skins he had to barter away for whatever he wanted (which may suggest the origins of the popularly-assumed oldest profession). It's the marketing process in vitro.

Now fast forward to the age of the ancient Greeks. By then, several millennia later, *Homo sapiens's* cerebrum had evolved into quite a sophisticated machine. As a consequence, these artistic, philosophical sons and daughters of Helen may have been, among other things, the first to consciously and extensively employ advertising. When grapes were harvested, tavern owners would display clusters of vine stems tied together over their doorways to graphically indicate that the wine was in and ready to drink. Get out the drachmas.

Going back to the beginnings, back to a time of raw fundamentals, we see that advertising is basically and essentially persuasion for profit. One advertises so that those qualities that the advertiser wants people to know concerning a product will in fact become known. If you think it through, understand the psychology of your market, and apply some imagination, like that Greek tavern owner who first thought of hanging out grapevines, you'll do more persuading and make more profit than your less-creative competition.

The Bottom Line

The common denominator of highly creative advertising is a concept built on a firm marketing base. Its effectiveness can be measured by how well it helps sell, not by how clever or outrageous it is. Cleverness and outrageousness can be well employed to help sell, but keep in mind they are not an end in themselves. You must constantly attend to the primary purpose of advertising, persuasion for profit. Your advertising agency can help suggest and design new products and product improvements. It can suggest new ways to approach your present markets, and new markets to approach. It can suggest and implement various research programs. Or you can do all or most of these things yourself. But what an agency or free-lance creative resource should be able to do better than you, and what it should be primarily concerned with, is the creation of attention-getting, persuasive advertising. Advertising that sells.

3

Three Ways To Get It Done

It is better to know some of the questions than all of the
answers.
—James Thurber

The case for working with a full-service, independent advertising agency can be a strong one. The fact is that most companies, certainly those with substantive and complex advertising needs, are best served by hiring corporately organized, objective professionals with the diversified skills needed to mount an effective advertising program. It is always tempting, particularly in this era of extreme cost consciousness, to think about doing it yourself. So we'll first consider the case for an independent advertising agency instead of the in-house alternative, and then we'll examine the intriguing how and when of using free-lancers.

Why an Advertising Agency vs. In-House

An advertising agency's primary purpose is to produce a product, a highly creative product. Keep this firmly in mind. An agency's focus is not that of a service business, as it is often mistakenly characterized, but rather that of a workshop churning out print ads, television commercials, radio commercials, outdoor billboards, direct marketing materials, and all manner of sales-support materials. Certainly service may be a critical element in an agency's success, but its reason for being is not service. A 30-second television commercial, a four-color

25

magazine ad, a series of newspaper ads—that's what the agency's business should be all about. A tangible, custom-made product. Each time one of these products is created, it is in effect a reinvention of the wheel. That's why, more so than in almost any other business, the distinctiveness and ingenuity of each of these custom-created products is fundamental with regard to how well the advertiser's investment is being spent.

Never forget that we're seeking advertising that works. We want advertising that gets attention and gets remembered and has that extra competitive edge. Those who present the in-house case make two basic faulty assumptions: (1) the end result will be better advertising for the company, and (2) a considerable portion of the commissions and fees paid to an agency will be profitably directed internally. Too often (but not always, of course) the genesis of these rationalizations is the desire of an individual in the company to increase his or her own responsibilities. It's the classic empire-building syndrome.

Some Cost Considerations

Let's examine the latter assumption ("The commissions and fees paid to an agency will be profitably directed internally"). This is a financial minefield. The great majority of advertisers who decide to make their own advertising (and all the marketing, media, production, and creative decisions that are part of the whole process) quite dramatically, and naively, underestimate the bottom-line consequences of doing so. They just don't analyze anywhere nearly enough (if they sharp pencil it at all) the heavy budget support that an in-house agency demands. First of all, some pretty sophisticated outside help is usually needed. One must be realistic about the number of people required, the level of the specialized skills they must have, and the range of the salaries necessary to attract and keep a reasonably qualified staff. Also, don't forget that as much as a quarter of their base salaries will be needed, above and beyond the salaries themselves, to pay for the employees' housing, supplies and equipment, and fringe benefits packages. It's one underestimation after another. And if you're really going to take a let's-not-kid-ourselves approach to the total impact of such a commitment, you'll factor in some healthy dollops of top officers' management time, an inevitable by-product of an in-house operation.

After all the arithmetic, the do-it-yourself advertiser may soon feel like the first-time homeowner who discovers the foundation needs shoring up, the roof leaks, the oil and electric bills come every month, the lawn needs weed killer, lime, and fertilizer, and the town is doubling the real estate tax. It's not just a mortgage number versus a rent number.

Some Creative Considerations

Now we're at the heart of the matter. The other assumption is "the end result will be better advertising for the company." But look at it this way; if you needed a triple bypass, would you rather rely on the professionals at Mass General or the company nurse? An extreme example perhaps, but we are talking about the life and growth of your company.

Our goal, remember, is highly creative, highy effective advertising. And, as we all know, advertising that works especially hard is not that easy to wring out of even the best independent agencies. As for in-house agencies, they aren't even in the stadium. They're playing a pickup game on a sandlot. Forget the happy accidents and the rare exceptions. In-house agencies, by their very single-focus nature, giving their total concentration to the one product (or group of related products) being advertised, inevitably fall short on breadth of experience, aggressiveness, objectivity, and freewheeling inventiveness—all very desirable if not essential professional qualities that lead to highly competitive, creative advertising.

There are certain businesses and certain circumstances that do call for an in-house advertising and promotion operation. In almost all these cases the most effective way to use such an operation is to put the group's emphasis on the promotion areas. These situations, however, are exceptions to the rule. As Ron Stander's wife put it, after her husband was quickly disposed of by Joe Frazier in the boxing ring, "If you're going to enter the Indianapolis 500 with a Volkswagen, you better know a hell of a shortcut."

When an In-House Agency Can Make Sense

One notable exception to my conviction that independent advertising agencies are far more effective than in-house units is the advertising and promotion departments set up at some of the larger retail stores. These departments can make sense because the advertising for a department store, for example, is extremely oriented toward fast-changing situations and new products. It is fast close; week in, week out; and highly market sensitive. Changes can often be made to good advantage literally hours before press time. In the fashion field—and much of a department store's focus is on fashion—what's hot and what's not can change almost as fast as it takes the escalator to get from street level to the fourth floor. The need to go beyond price and position a product as up-to-the-minute is extremely important. The department staff, both buyers and promotion people, live and breathe trends every waking moment. They are constantly traveling and talking to designers and manufacturers in the industry and can play back to their own people the needs of the moment. And for all in-store departments, besides advertising in newspapers, magazines, radio, and TV, there are often a myriad of fliers, brochures, bill stuffers, in-store posters, and special-event promotion materials that need to be churned out week after week.

For these reasons, and because there is far less pressure for highly creative concepts, and because there may be many ads for different departments on the same day, much retail advertising is put together by an in-house promotion staff. (One example is The Gap, a fashion-directed retailer-designer, that has its own in-house group producing its advertising and promotion material.) If you look at the retail advertising in your daily newspaper, listen to it on your local radio, or see it on TV, you'll see it has a style all its own. Show the product, give the price, inject a sense of urgency (On Sale Now!). It's somewhat formularized, with its own creative character, and it often works very well.

Typically, some other companies that have felt that in-house agencies offer them advantages have been cosmetics houses. Revlon, for instance, gave a former agency owner–creative director the responsibility of creating all their advertising and promotion materials in-house. And many industrial companies have traditionally created most of their promotion materials in-house, supplementing these operations with outside agencies for their advertising needs.

Radio and TV stations and, even more so, magazine and newspaper publishers tend to have substantive in-house promotion staffs. These companies usually have the staff handle mailing pieces and sales aids, and assign their advertising agencies the creation of their trade (advertising promotion) and consumer (circulation promotion) campaigns.

How Bloomingdale's In-House Agency Is Structured

One of the premier in-house agency operations is that of New York's world-famous Bloomingdale's. The house agency's clients are the 110 buyers in the store, all of whom have needs for advertising and promotion materials, either regularly or from time to time. The product areas range from furniture to fashion to everything Bloomingdale's sells.

There are some 40 people in the sales promotion group. Within the group there is a senior vice president, John Jay, who is the creative director for Advertising and Design. There are 4 art directors, 7 copywriters, 3 stylists, 3 media expediters, and some 20 production people (to ensure the completion of the film needs and mechanicals for the printers, magazines, and news- papers). The responsibilities of the group include advertising, direct mail, direct response, public relations, and packaging.

A full-service, independent agency is retained as well to develop all of Bloomingdale's television commercials. The ideas come from both Bloomingdale's and the agency people, but the agency produces the spots.

However, even in such an unstable, pulse-taking industry as fashion, a company might well look to farming out as much work as is practical to free-lancers or to a retained advertising agency, both for economy and for fresh thinking. A good example of a company that has done this is Calvin Klein. For a number of years a lean inside staff has produced their advertising. The inspiration for much of it came from the very creative Mr. Klein himself. The advertising was often controversial and always got attention, largely because the client was willing to take risks. The inside staff was, however, supported by some very talented free-lance support people. Recently an advertising agency was retained as well.

In all these examples, I'm convinced that leaner staffs working with free-lancers or independent advertising agencies would result in more effective advertising and promotion materials at greater cost efficiency. But there are exceptions.

Making Ads Without an Advertising Agency

A company with a relatively modest, reasonably uncomplicated advertising program might well consider the use of free-lancers. Free-lancers come in all shapes and sizes. There are copywriters and art directors (who focus on print and TV advertising) and graphic designers (whose main skill is in designing brochures, posters, and logos). There are marketing people, media people, production people (some specializing in TV and radio, others in print)—literally every conceivable matchup with a specialist in an advertising agency structure. Some of these free-lancers are at it full-time, preferring the more free-form, emotionally charged life of the entrepreneur. Some are moonlighters, working at an agency by day and on your project by night. In either case, if you put one of them to work for you, be sure to check out any conflicts of interest.

Some of the most talented free-lancers are quite successful at handling a broad range of assignments. Others tend to be very specialized. One may concentrate on fashion and beauty; another may work on only financial, automotive, or pharmaceutical ads. Some copy free-lancers have a knack for radio or television, or humor, or positioning lines. One art director may be especially adept at editorial-type layouts with long copy, and another may excel at bold, gutsy layouts. You have to know your free-lancer's strength. If you find an especially talented, multipurpose writer and art director, hang on tight. Keep good free-lancers happy. They'll get to know your company, your products, and you and will be able to react to any number of needs quickly and on target, saving you time and money.

Qualities to Look for in Free-Lancers

Copywriter: Look for a clear, direct thinker who can grasp the premise and translate it into relevant copy that is persuasive to the target market. An advertising writer, as opposed to most other writing professionals, must be strong on concept. He or she must present the central idea in a few words. The headline and visual must connect strongly with the ad's objective.

Art director: Obviously the art director (or graphic designer, when the layout and design are concerned with other than a print ad or TV commercial) and the copywriter must be on the same wavelength as to the fundamental concept. The art director has to present the words and any illustrations or photos in a way that fits the concept, as well as the character of the company. Look for examples of previous work that are inviting and easy to read. The idea is to communicate and persuade.

Media professionals: The objective is to choose media appropriate to the target market; you want to reach that market as efficiently as possible. Work with people you can understand. You don't want people who will intimidate you with technical terms. Be sure they have at their fingertips computers that are keyed in to a number of data banks. Be sure those data banks are large enough to insure that the media professionals are buying broadly across a number of different mediums. You want people who are up on the latest in all the markets you will be addressing.

The key to using free-lancers is that the company staff who interface with them must have tact, sensitivity, and a motivational flair when working with gifted people—the ones you want to have doing your work. Such staff people must be open-minded and have a sure grasp of the purpose of the advertising. And that purpose must be clearly communicated to the free-lancer. Creative types are most creative when they know what to be creative about.

The staff person will oversee and set the course for the development of the advertising, essentially in the same manner as an account manager at an independent agency. In fact, when you staff the position, consider a knowledgeable, broadly based account person from an agency. In any case be sure that the person to whom you give the responsibility has both a thorough knowledge of advertising and, in particular, the authority to make decisions. Otherwise, nothing much will get done, and that which is done will be worried out of its power and bite.

No matter how you do it, the ultimate objective is to get powerful, effective advertising. The readers of your advertising message won't even think about whether the ad was created in a week by one person or over three months by a group of six people at the largest agency in the world after four committee reviews and seven very vocal debates. Obviously, the more easily and quickly you produce a superior piece of advertising, the more cost-effective it will be. If you're going the free-lance route, be consistent all the way. Structure a lean, smart internal setup to supervise and push matters along. The people you want interfacing with free-lancers should be, first and foremost, intelligent and, second, knowledgeable about advertising. They should not be copy or art people who are going to stick their fingers into every assignment. Rather, put make-it-happen, keep-it-moving managers on the job. With the right free-lance network in place, the various needs can be delegated out with the commission to "go do it." First try a staff interface with one assistant. See if your company needs can be met by that tight a staffing. Add one or two if need be, as experience and practicality dictate. The economic advantages of free-lance talent will be lost if you start enlisting a small army to manage it. You'll be getting into building your own in-house agency; and that, I say with passionate conviction, is, with a few exceptions, the worst of all worlds.

The Bottom Line

What it all comes down to is that exceptionally effective advertising is born of exceptionally gifted, creative people. Look for itchy, irrepressible, restless people of unfettered imagination and daring who thrive on the broad range of challenges posed by creating advertising for so many different kinds of products. Individuals who have created scores and scores of ads, in all shapes and forms—TV commercials, print ads, posters—can give you a smorgasbord of advertising experience. It results in a cross-fertilization of know-how from the various sales and marketing approaches of all the many different industries served. You get a relentless creative effort that gets high visibility, won't let people rest on their laurels, and keeps egos charged up and bubbling.

If your needs demand an agency (and probably most companies will benefit from one) resist the temptation to create an in-house agency. Your objective is advertising that works, not creating a staff on whom the sun never sets. Consider first a very lean inside staff with a broad understanding of all phases of the advertising industry, supplemented by a highly talented core of creative support professionals. For more complex accounts, an advertising agency can be an important part of the mix. But even the largest advertisers, employing mega-agencies, can benefit greatly in cost savings and the generation of innovative, hardworking, creative ideas by looking to a free-lance resource as well.

The fact of the matter, born of experience, is that independent advertising agencies or free-lance situations offer the principal opportunities for the most talented copywriters and art directors to do their thing. And that's how you get sizzle.

As a starting point, try a staff interface with one assistant, adding more if necessary. Use free-lancers if your program is relatively straightforward. If it is a large, complex program, by all means go for an independent agency. Just make sure you know how the advertising agency works and how to get the most out of it. We'll see how to do this next.

4

How An Agency Works

He who does not know the mechanical side of a craft
cannot judge it.
—Goethe

If you plan on gathering honey from the hive, you better understand bee behavior and how the colony is organized. Likewise, understanding the whys and wherefores of agency busyness will help you know how to wring top-notch creativity (the royal jelly, so to speak) out of them. So we'll take a look at who is supposed to do what at the agency, and what you should know about the responsibilities of the people in the key areas.

Before anything else, though, remember this. In entrusting your company's advertising to an agency, you expect that they will plan, create, and realize the advertising you need to support your sales effort. Getting the right matchup is important, because the whole process is only going to work if you interact closely and openly with the group while giving them the elbow room to do their thing for you. So be sure you understand and are comfortable with the corporate culture, the corporate personality of the group you are working with. People chemistry and being on a similar philosophical wavelength is critical.

Sizing Up an Agency's Character

Some agencies believe so fervently in their creative judgment that they underestimate the client's market savvy and judgment. They won't let go of the bone. They doggedly insist on everything being their way.

35

On the other hand, there are agencies who have gone to client-obedience school. They roll over and play dead. They lack the courage and fortitude to retain their independent, third-party perspective and don't push hard enough with reasoned, forceful arguments for what they are convinced will make for better advertising.

Either way you will end up being shortchanged. But take note that the latter can be more dangerous than the former. If you are deadly serious about action-provoking creativity, you'll have to guard against being intimidating. Too many clients fail to appreciate the potential impact of a creative proposal and unwittingly force their agencies into executing bland, familiar, "safe" advertising—exactly what you should not be looking for from your agency.

Also, remember that just as you can't be all things to all people, neither can an agency. Some agencies may produce outstanding advertising for one type of client and be woefully incapable of creatively coming to grips with the needs of another. Be certain that the style of your agency, no matter how hot their reputation, is appropriate to and effective for your business.

Sizing Up an Agency's Management

Clients tend to be most comfortable with the management people at agencies. They do those kinds of things, like hitting golf balls and tennis balls, that the clients themselves do; clients can hardly tell them apart from the company staff. Almost invariably those who dress like clients are the account people, and those who dress like it's Saturday are the creative people. The creative people, as clients see it, are at the least unconventional and at the most downright flaky.

It's because of this perception, which has just enough of the ring of truth to be taken as gospel, that the burden is on agency management to establish rapport with you and the other people from your firm they work with. Attention and responsiveness are basic to the relationship. If the people you sit down with on a day-to-day basis are not giving you these things, then above and beyond any creative considerations, you know that you're not only in the wrong pew, you're in the wrong church. Keeping you, the client, satisfied is after all absolutely and totally essential to the business success of the advertising agency. A successful client-agency relationship is built on meticulous, fervid account management and regular top management involvement.

Let's look at the individual parts of the agency, what they mean to you, and how you can help insure that they are working to give you the most compelling advertising possible.

Managing Your Account

The account executive has the buck-stops-here responsibility for client contact and for coordinating, initiating, and authorizing all the marketing, media, and creative work within the agency for that account. You want your doctor to be the smartest, most knowledgeable, best diagnostician (with a little bedside manner thrown in), right? The same goes for your account executive.

A client may be serviced by a group dedicated exclusively to the account or be one of several accounts brought together in an account group. The account manager (or, depending on the agency nomenclature, the account director or management supervisor) is the one in charge of all accounts in a group. Account executives (or account supervisors) are those with the day-to-day working responsibility on a specific account. Again, depending on the agency, the terminology may vary, but there is always some such hierarchy. And, in some cases, the head of the agency, if a professional account manager, might personally take on the day-to-day handling of an account that is critical to the agency's success.

Whatever the titles, the most productive account people are those who happily and aggressively live in two worlds, the world of the client and the world of the agency. Their job, to oversimplify a little, is to have a sympathetic feeling for and thorough understanding of both.

Understanding Your Business

There are some fundamentals to knowing the client. An important, basic point is that all account people should have read their client's annual report as a beginning step. It's incredible how many have not. Someone should, if at all feasible, make some calls with a salesperson. And the account people should thoroughly investigate what the competition is up to. Account management begins with a thorough knowledge of the client company, the personalities who make it up, its products, strengths, operations, markets, problems, and competition. Call it Client 101.

All this intelligence must be translated into how to best help the client company achieve its objectives. To succeed at this, the account person helps formulate the basic advertising strategy recommended by the agency (sometimes with the help of an account planner, whose function is discussed later in this chapter), makes sure that the suggested advertising is on target, and presents (with appropriate specialists he or she may call on) the proposal—media schedules, budget, and rough layouts of print ads or storyboards of TV commercials—to the client for approval. Then comes the tricky part. Once the proposal is approved, with whatever fine-tunings and adjustments, there's the task of making sure that the agency actually delivers the final product as promised and that the client is kept sold on the validity and quality of the agreed-upon approach.

In fulfilling the people-sensitive demands of the job—being the liaison between the agency and the client, helping to formulate direction, seeing to it that the agency sticks to the objectives, explaining the client's point of view to the agency and the agency's point of view to the client—heaping amounts of diplomacy and tact are needed, as well as, sometimes, a little Pepto-Bismol.

Understanding the Agency's Business

To make things happen back at the shop, it's essential for an account person to know how to get things done through the formal structure: the forms and procedures and administrative nitty-gritty that must be meticulously kept up-to-the-minute. There is the coordinating of creative, production, and media schedules. There are the critical needs of holding a tight rein on costs all along the way and seeing that both billing and bill paying are handled expeditiously. The account person must keep things moving on schedule on an account, in spite of the agency's groaning work load and all the other deadline priorities competing for time and attention.

In making all this happen, the account person needs to have the dexterity, initiative, and smarts to get things done outside the formal structure as well. There's a lot of stroking, filling in, and drawing out that needs doing with a very diverse cast of characters. The responsible account person must constantly provoke action so as to keep the agency several steps ahead of the client's needs. Certainly he or she must be an articulate and enthusiastic advocate of the agency's work and its strengths and must serve as a catalyst (a cheerleader, a prodder, a psychiatrist, and even a mother) in bringing out the best in the agency's creative talent. Obviously the job profile for an account person calls for a slick-tongued charmer, highly skilled in one-on-one communication, who's a detail-oriented workaholic.

Making the Ad

You've been there. The atmosphere is elegant, the waiters are attentive, and the candlelight flickers off the wineglasses. Unfortunately, the food is lousy. If the lead account person is the maître d', then the creative director is the chef. After all, an advertising agency's main course is the creative product. If your agency gives you inspired marketing, intelligent media planning, and precise account management but produces indifferent advertising, what you'll have at best is a one-star agency.

On the other hand, an agency that serves up absolutely wonderful, hardworking advertising is, even though its marketing support, media planning, and account management may only be a notch above fair to middling, an agency to be appreciatively savored.

This does not mean that everything other than exceptionally creative advertising is unimportant. It does mean that if all the other services and functions are at least adequate, and you have sizzling, shout-hallelujah creativity, you're cooking on the front burner. Creativity must be the pièce de résistance. You can't afford to be dazzled and distracted by the other elements, as important as they may be. As noted earlier, the ultimate reader or viewer of your message knows nothing about who created it, the steps it took to get there, whether it came from a big or small agency, or how the client's CEO liked it. All he or she knows is that it does or doesn't strike a responsive chord. (But if, Heaven be praised, all else as well as the creative is breathtakingly superb, call the *Guinness Book of Records*. Better yet, call a local priest. He may put forward a petition to Rome to have a miracle proclaimed.)

The point is that you must focus on the end product. It's what it's all about. Some time back Booz Allen & Hamilton did a classic study for the Association of National Advertisers. One of the most significant statements in the report was that, according to their findings, a superior advertising idea could be as much as ten times more effective than an ordinary idea; ten times more bang for the buck. Even if the ratio were only five to one, the implication of this is enough to make one sprint, not lollygag along, to the Creative Zone.

Copywriter and Art Director

The creative department of an advertising agency is essentially made up of copywriters and art directors. Usually the group is led by a creative director. The creative director could have come up through either copy or art. Depending on the size of the agency or the size of your budget or both, the creative director may actually be the copy or art person working directly on your account. Larger creative departments may have associate creative directors, copy chiefs, group heads, or other titles designed to bring some bite size structure to the department. Whatever patterns and labels the particular organizational boxes take, accounts are assigned so that the work of conceiving, developing, and creating the advertising is done by a team of a copywriter and an art director. The creative hierarchy may or may not be intimately involved, in spite of what you may have been promised. Be that as it may, your most urgent concern should be with just how gifted and experienced are the copywriter-and-art-director team or teams assigned to you.

In shaping the direction of the end product, the intelligent agency will include an appropriate mix of copy, art, and account people. At some point the copywriter and art director will get to spend some quiet time apart, crafting the concept and words and shaping the overall message and feel of the particular piece, whether for print or TV. Each will feed the other, making adjustments so that the concept is presented in the most compelling manner. There are no absolutes; but because advertising is such a concept-driven art, you can pretty much take as gospel that the best copywriters think visually as well as verbally, and the best art directors think verbally as well as visually. The fact is that many a visual approach was born in the mind of a copywriter, just as many a headline is the child of an art director.

In fairness, it should be noted that there have been many instances when an account manager has had the inspiration. And there have been instances when clients have lit the light bulb. It shouldn't matter to professionals whose idea it is, just as long as there is one super sizzler to work with. Recognizing a good idea is as important as conceiving one, which is a primary concern of this book. Wherever an idea originates, it is the ultimate responsibility of the copy-and-art team to work the idea through to the finished ad.

Of course, in the crafting of a TV or radio commercial, a key player is the director. More often than not, the creative concept is completed and the copy and visual concept have been worked out by the copywriter and art director (and any others who were involved in the process) before the director makes it all happen. But sometimes the director has a vision that alters the idea slightly or even dramatically, with happy creative consequences.

The crux of the matter is people. As one legendary advertising agency executive put it, "My inventory goes down the elevator every night." Fundamental to a successful, highly creative advertising agency are gifted, creative, conceptually oriented people, whether copywriters, art directors, or account managers.

Conceptual orientation is the make-or-break quality. It is not enough, for example, to be a good writer. Novelists, newspaper reporters, poets, no matter how accomplished in their field, may be totally incapable of translating their writing skills into superior advertising ideas and copy. Nor will a successful painter necessarily be able to make strong advertising layouts. (Unfortunately, if the plethora of mediocre advertising is an indication, the same can be said for too many plying their copy and art skills in the advertising business today. Genius, in advertising no less than in other fields, is a delicate and rare orchid.)

Being an exceptionally effective copywriter or art director depends on a couple of things. Certainly it demands that one learn how to think on the sales wavelength. That discipline alone can insure a moderately clever person a rather decent-paying career. Second, and most critical, are good genes. A person can work at painting for an entire lifetime and never become a Picasso. Another can practice, practice, practice at the keyboard and never become a Horowitz.

However and whyever it happens, some people in advertising have an inner vision of what makes the world work the way it does. They are able to persuasively reflect that vision in two-dimensional space or in 30 seconds on TV. That gift, along with learning how to think on the selling/persuasion wavelength, can insure a truly talented person a very, very decent-paying career.

Knowing who has it and who doesn't is a dicey business, and a critical one for an advertiser. It's not always obvious; as one wag put it, "Some of the prettiest girls don't kiss very well." A particular creative person may have a reputation of heroic proportions and be touted as a knight in shining armor. Just be sure you find out when the person's magnificent white horse was last shod. Some copywriters and art directors deserve their exalted position, and others are in the same league as the Wizard of Oz. If your ads and commercials, one after another, have selling propositions that catch interest, with clear, convincing language, then maybe, just maybe, you've got a copywriter blessed with the touch. And if an art director's work for you is consistently arresting and makes its point almost at a glance, with inviting, easy-to-read copy and a graphic structure (either type, photograph, illustration, or some combination of elements) with a strong focal point, then maybe, just maybe, you've got yourself a dynamic duo. Tell your account person that it's OK to let an insertion date slip by now and then or, once in a great while, to screw up a bill or even to be late, real late, for lunch one day. These things happen to the best of us. Just make sure that he or she sees to it that nothing less than a brilliant, conceptually minded copywriter-and-art-director team is assigned to your account. Without the conceptual brilliance, you'll be without the sizzle.

The Account Planner

I like to think, as unlikely as it may be, that I had something to do with inspiring the idea of the account planner. A man named Stanley Pollit shaped the concept and integrated the position into his advertising agency structure, and thus into the British approach to advertising, in the mid-1960s. Just prior to this time, very early on in my career, I was assigned to work in London; and in each of the three years I was there,

I won the top award from the British Direct Marketing Association, twice for best single piece and once for best campaign. I made a number of speeches to various advertising groups, and in one speech I described myself as not so much a copywriter than as a sociologist and psychologist. The point was that to create outstanding advertising, one must understand both the sociological factors affecting a specific market and the psychological factors affecting individuals within the frame of reference. In other words, I preached, get into the shoes of your prospects. This is the essence of account planning.

A number of American agencies have recently introduced the account planner into their agencies. The account planner's role is to represent the customer. Planners are not concerned with budgets, media schedules, timetables, and day-to-day client contact, as are account people. Neither are they concerned with executing copy, photography, typography, or commercial production. Their responsibility is to understand how potential customers are thinking; to know as much as possible about their attitudes and perceptions; to come to a conclusion about which appeals will turn customers on and which appeals will have little or no impact.

The account planner is essentially a researcher who interacts with the customer. He or she does not use the more historically employed system of quantitative research but rather qualitative research (see the section "Marketing and Research," which is next). The account planner conducts in-person interviews in malls, on the street, in offices, and in the home; telephone interviews; and focus groups. Focus group sessions use the time-honored procedure of inviting about 10 typical customers into a room and having an in-depth discussion about the product, competitive products, and the participants' feelings and needs concerning them.

All the responses and impressions are interpreted by the planner, and an analysis of what they mean and how to address customers' state of mind is presented, as objectively as possible, to the creative people charged with developing the advertising approach. The gifted account planner, by intelligently and intuitively describing the mind-set of the targeted market, can be a critical catalyst in the creation of an effective advertising appeal. Knowing what to be creative about is the key to making advertising that works.

Two points need to be made. First, the skill and talent of the individual, just as in any professional role, is critical in performing the task well: in the case of the account planner, obtaining on-target information and opinions. Second, this process has been operative among account and creative people from time immemorial in creating outstanding advertising. Putting yourself into the customers' shoes and acting as a sociologist and psychologist have always been essential in creating advertising that works. The advantage of building an account planner's function into the modus operandi of an agency is that it insures that the procedure is being followed, and that advertising is not being created by raw instinct and gut feel alone.

Marketing and Research

A buttoned-up, charmingly persuasive account manager, who knows what it's all about and can make things happen, and a conceptually brilliant copy-and-art team are fundamental in delivering advertising built on a sound marketing position that will strike the right chord with your targeted markets. But a conductor's baton is not a magic wand. Even Leonard Bernstein needed great musicians to back up all that arm waving. There are some other players who, though not front row soloists, are critical in making the whole thing come off harmoniously.

It's the account manager's job to keep everyone moving along together, measure by measure, pointing (so to speak) now at the strings, now at the brass, now at the percussion. The starting point for so doing, to extend the metaphor (and as emphasized earlier), is knowing the score. Before preparing any advertising, the most important consideration is understanding what it is supposed to do. The objective must, of course, be realistic. In judging how much the advertising can reasonably be expected to do, an understanding of current economic and societal trends and the company's products, distribution system, competitive situation, and future plans is essential.

So all along the way, we must attend to marketing. Historically a market is, as we noted before, a place where things are sold. Marketing, in the best of all worlds, is concerned with the buyer's needs and desires. The best copy and art people take their understandings of the world and intuitively play to those needs and desires.

The best account people are more formally marketing-oriented in their training and outlook. Whether or not there are specific and specialized marketing people or account planning people or both involved depends on the nature and needs of the client and the structure of the agency. What is essential, in all cases, is that the account person has a strong marketing focus that can be effectively fed to the creative team.

Some basic, and often sufficient, market research can be accomplished through the resources within the agency. Or, because information gathering is such a specialized and esoteric profession, more elaborate research can be contracted for from an outside, independent research group. This process, too, is usually managed by the account person or, if the agency is so structured, by the research director or account planner. Any heavy-duty research is paid for by the client, which means the intent and process must be approved before the research begins. In almost every case, you can be sure that intelligently pinpointed research will, in the long haul, save both time and money.

Quantitative and Qualitative Information

It's not just, How many beans are in the jar? It's also, What do they taste like? Whatever sophisticated wrinkles are applied to a marketing research technique, it all comes down to two kinds of investigation: (1) quantitative research, which measures the numbers of things—how many or how much of what or who—and (2) qualitative research, which measures attitudes and perceptions—what people feel and think.

The information gained from either or both helps us to understand the target market and the forces that influence that market. At best the data will help build or confirm an understanding of the marketing position for the product being sold, against the current societal moment and vis-à-vis the competition.

Of course, research is a never-ending activity. There's information gathering that precedes the creation of the actual advertising, as just noted, and there are both ongoing benchmark and postevent studies. Depending on the nature of your company and your product, research can play a major or minimal role in the activity of the account.

The Media Department

Eventually, after all the information from research has been thought through and appropriately applied to shaping the advertising concept and all the creative thinking and execution has come to fruition in the form of a finished print ad or commercial, it's time to expose it to the prospect audience and put it to work. This is where the media people come in. These people are analytical and comfortable with detail work, conducting research, and working with computers and numbers. If they're good at things like chess, figuring out whodunit in mysteries, and solving jigsaw puzzles, it should not surprise you.

It's their job to determine where, when, how often, and for how long the finished creative products will appear in front of targeted prospects. The processes involved in answering these questions can be reasonably technical, and often complicated. But don't get thrown by the jargon and the flowcharts. As Tallulah Bankhead was known to observe, "There is less in this than meets the eye." Keep in mind that what it all gets down to is that a superior media plan should reach the greatest number of realistically targeted prospects within the given budget.

A clear description of those to whom the advertising is addressed is essential in crafting a plan. The account planner or research people or both, the client, and the account management people have to collaborate and be very specific about this description in order for the media planners to choose publications or radio and TV stations, and the specific shows and times on those stations to carry the advertising. Armed with specific descriptions, demographics, and goals, the more conscientious and deductively skillful will prepare a plan or set of plans that will use the money well.

Collecting Data

The choices of which publications and stations and times and so forth that make up a media plan are not made whimsically. A number of resources provide the hard data necessary to make the many decisions that go into shaping an effective plan. Information can be obtained through computer services that give a wealth of information about prospective readers, listeners, and viewers: sex, age, income, education level, where they live, what they read, what they watch, and so forth. All this information comes from independent sources, which collect and sell the data as a service, as well as the various advertising mediums themselves. Data from the latter are statistics about readers, viewers, or listeners from publications and stations, putting their best foot forward to make the sale. This is not to say that the facts and figures are not useful or reliable, but they are not impartial and must be considered in light of the information provided from competitive sources and the independent data services.

One more point regarding media selection: when all the data are collected and the cold numbers suggest a conclusion as to which publications or TV and radio stations to use, it's time to add a few dollops of gut feel and prejudice. If you think the programming on a particular station is more suited to your product and your view of yourself, or that the overall character of *Alpha* magazine is more in tune with your message than is the character of *Beta* magazine, throw those instinctive judgments into the mix. Never ignore the message of your third ear. But don't be foolish. If the gap between your own prejudices and what the numbers are telling you is marked, go with what the numbers are telling you. That's the objective, hard-nosed value of careful and thorough professional media analysis.

Negotiating the Best Prices

Selection decisions are the bedrock of a well-targeted media plan. Negotiation with those advertising mediums that are selected is where we separate the champs from the chumps. Intelligently and aggressively negotiated rates can extend the reach of your budget by up to 30 percent to 50 percent. Broadcast, both television and radio, has traditionally been like a Persian rug market, with enormous swings in what a given advertiser might pay for time. It's like traveling on an airline. If you ask your traveling companion what he or she paid for that seat, chances are that you'll find you each paid widely different rates. There are no fixed rates or rate cards in broadcast, and sorting out what's the right price, or how many spots you'll get for the same price and when, is a nightmare that takes great skill, diplomacy, knowledge, and patience to work to your advantage. Even print mediums, magazines and newspapers, who had sometimes been very rigid about their prices and who published cast-in-concrete rate cards, now tend to use negotiable pricing.

Big vs. Small vs. Independent

How do you know your agency is getting the job done in these areas? Well, it's not easy. But in general you can be sure that the bigger agencies will have more clout with the media than the smaller ones. They place more advertising, and the various publications and stations are going to work cooperatively with them to win more and more business. Besides which, they have firsthand, up-to-date knowledge of the best current market prices. However, a smaller agency can even the playing field by working through an independent media planning and buying service, a specialized company that does nothing but plan and buy media for agencies and advertisers directly. Even some larger agencies have decided to use these companies as a supplement to their own media department or, in some cases, to do all their media planning and buying.

If your agency uses a media planning and buying service, depending on the nature of your account and the complexity of the media buy, they will pay the media company a portion of their earned commission. For buys in the spot broadcast area that do not include a whole national network, but entail market-by-market choices and negotiations, a superior service can often buy at advantageous rates, and the percentage of the commission due them will frequently be paid by the advertiser on top of the full commission to the agency. As the spot broadcast budget gets bigger, say, $5 million and over, the income to the agency might be big enough that the client would expect the agency to give up part of its commission to compensate the media service. The advantage to the client of paying the percentage is that it encourages the agency to use such a specialized service, gaining the negotiating advantage, rather than trying to protect its full commission.

A Word on Legal

I'm not going to tell you that every single thing that goes out with your name on it in the way of a print advertisement or television or radio commercial must be passed by legal eyes. There are those who say that everything should, and they're not necessarily wrong. But much is similar enough to previously approved material that experienced account management people know that it does not in any way pose a risk. However, in today's litigious society, where rules quickly change and precedents are set every week, a legal sign-off of any material that will be seen by any audience is somewhere between prudent and essential.

Large agencies will have their own legal department, consisting of one or more people. Be advised that having a law degree is not qualification enough for the job. A thorough understanding of advertising law, broadcast law, use of celebrities, risks inherent in claims, and union regulations concerning actors, directors, photographers, and so on is essential to doing the job in a manner that protects the client and the agency.

Some independent law firms have a department that specializes in advertising law. They can be employed on an as-needed basis, usually with a monthly retainer. All prudent small agencies should have such an arrangement in place. Here again, many larger agencies are opting to contract for these services rather than have an in-house legal department. The advantage for them, as for the smaller agencies, which can only afford to work this way, is that independent firms see a broader picture because of the increased diversity and volume that they are exposed to, and the agencies pay just for those services as required. Incidentally, it is appropriate for legal charges to be billed to the client. As with any charge, your agency should get a sign-off on estimated costs. However, the large revenue-producing accounts may well expect that these costs be borne by the agency itself.

Traffic, Production, and the Go-Between

There are a few other types in the pits, changing the tires and keeping the gas tank full, who are, on a day-to-day basis, very important to you. And again it is the account person who keeps them in gear and firing on all cylinders.

The traffic manager is the one on roller skates going from desk to desk to drawing board, checking on where everything is at. As the name implies, this function requires a person with a conscientious, follow-up-and-follow-through mentality. Being a traffic manager means knowing where each job stands in the development chain and knowing when it must be at the next stage. It means starting with the due date of the material and progressively scheduling backwards, allowing enough time to complete each step, taking unforeseen glitches into account, to insure making the deadline.

Hand in hand with the traffic manager is the production manager. In fact, in smaller agencies, the jobs are more often than not combined. The print production manager has to see to and contract out all the production needs—typography, photography, retouching, film manufacturing (in what sizes and to what exact specifications the media must have). The broadcast production manager (usually called a producer) is concerned with casting and booking talent, calling in reels of directors and production companies and choosing which among them will be contracted to do the job, and arranging for studios, editing, and music. Here again, this person works backwards from the absolutely inflexible date when the finished commercial must be delivered to the stations, through all the complexities of the step-by-step scheduling, in close and intimate collaboration with the account manager.

There are a number of other people behind the scenes who are important to realizing the goal of sizzling creativity. There are collateral and sales promotion specialists, audiovisual people, and the accounting department. And certainly don't forget the secretary, or assistant, who serves as the go-between, keeping in frequent telephone contact with you, arranging for things to be faxed or messengered, and tracking down the account manager, copywriter, or art director for any and all needs. The importance an agency places on filling this position, no less than all others, with a crackerjack, will tell you a lot about the agency's commitment to quality.

The Bottom Line

Know how your agency is structured and what procedures they prefer to best get the job done. But look to the philosophy of agency leadership; the tone and character of an agency is set at the top. Remember the big three we've been talking about—your account manager, your copywriter, your art director. If these elements are on target, you've got a good chance to get some superior, highly creative advertising.

So if you're ready to hone to a fine edge your ability to recognize what is and what isn't highly compelling, effective advertising, let's move into the Creative Zone.

SECTION TWO
Welcome to the Creative Zone

As you enter the Creative Zone, remember that an appreciation of what sizzles and what doesn't begins with knowledge and experience. Understand how the creative process works, your own creative capacity, and, very, very importantly, the artistic temperament of those who will be shaping your advertising.

There is something commanding and persuasive about the positive and decisive creative personality. Indeed, a creator must believe in his or her work. This is where you will be walking a tightrope, for you must criticize if you are to judge; at the same time, the creator's own conviction and enthusiasm for a concept can be unwarrantedly shaken by the inflexibly negative person. Neither encourage those who constantly and narrowly defend their ideas to the death nor those who let others pick apart every idea they present. Nor should you yourself go to these extremes. As John Kenneth Galbraith put it, "When people are least sure, they are often most dogmatic."

5

The Five-and-a-Half Minute Guide To Creativity

Explanation separates us from astonishment, which is the
only gateway to the incomprehensible.
—Ionesco

Take a few minutes to go over the very basic brain facts that follow, information that you well may know. Thinking about thinking seems to provide a jolt that carries over into how we perform as thinkers. So by way of review, let's think about how we think.

Anatomically the brain has three major parts, the hindbrain, the midbrain, and the forebrain. Our primary interest is with the forebrain, which includes the cerebral hemispheres—those much–talked-about left and right hemispheres. The left hemisphere is where you're at now. It's the area that processes information. It's analytic, sequential, and rational. The right hemisphere picks up on this information and, so to speak, holds it up to the light. It is visual-spatial, intuitive, and visionary. It's this right hemisphere that helps us make those inspired "Hey, I got it!" creative leaps. (Some recent evidence, however, suggests that both hemispheres contribute to processes that had previously been attributed to each one separately.)

All in all the human brain is only one-fourth as big as an elephant's brain and one-seventh as big as a whale's brain. It's our cerebral cortexes, the upper portion of our cerebrums, that give us the intellectual edge. The human cerebral cortex, the seat of memory,

55

learning, and abstract thinking, is far larger than that of any other mammal. From an evolutionary point of view, the cerebral cortex is the newest and largest region in the human brain, making up 90 percent of its mass. In fact, if you were to flatten out all its wrinkles and convoluted folds, which allow it to fit within the skull, it would spread out to about the size of a bath towel. You can appreciate the significance of this when you consider that the brain contains about 100 billion neurons and 1,000 trillion circuit connections and that 70 percent of this circuitry is in the cerebral cortex. This should emphasize the fact that the brain has an astronomical number of pathways through its cells, with the result that any neuron or group of neurons can contact a myriad number of other neurons through its trillions and trillions of circuits. It seems there is no excuse for not being original.

You Lost 100,000 Brain Cells Today

The bad news is that you're losing approximately 100,000 brain cells a day, due to aging. Count the days just since you started school, and multiply by 100,000; the figure will certainly be a staggering one. But no need to panic or fret. The good news is that over 60 years, we lose only a little over 2 percent of all the cells. Remember, there are some 100 billion neurons in the brain, and a happy feature of that gray-and-white lump is its redundancy, which means that the same information is stored in more than one place. We are not, with those 100,000 lost neurons each day, necessarily being deprived of knowledge that is unavailable to us elsewhere.

Even so, as we get older we do notice what seems to be some loss of memory. More than likely this is just a result of both more and more information stored over time and longer retrieval time (which is not to say we remember everything). The brain is quite discriminating about holding on to what it has processed. It stores information in two basic modes, short-term memory and long-term memory. Selective forgetting occurs with short-term memory. What is more interesting and relevant is sorted out and stored in long-term memory.

Your Brain Fingerprint

People are different physiologically. Patrick Ewing is significantly taller than Michael J. Fox. Genetically some people are quicker, stronger, or more agile than others. So, too, are the neural pathways in Stephen Hawking's brain of a different sort than those of the Jukes and Kallikaks, or yours or mine. What we can do, whatever the neural structure of our brain, is take what we've got, understand it, and develop habits and techniques to optimize its output.

To complicate our quest for especially effective ideas, there is no generally accepted theory of creativity. Nor is there a consensus as to how best scientifically investigate it. However, it's fair to say that most researchers in the field define creativity as a product of unconscious cerebration that somehow emerges into the light of consciousness. So there's a beginning.

The Creative Process

If exactly what takes place in the dark, internal folds of the brain before an idea emerges remains unknown, what has been quite thoroughly and diligently observed are these four steps in the creative process:

1. The creative act begins with a period of study, a gathering of facts, a conscious effort of creation or problem solving.

2. This is invariably followed by misdirected attention, frustration, or fatigue. The materials can then go beyond the conscious to the unconscious to be worked over, whether for a matter of seconds or years.

3. After this incubation period, the thought breaks through into consciousness, either as a growing awareness or in a sudden flash of perception.

4. Finally, there is verification, testing, checking out the details, and developing the concept.

The first and last steps of this four-level process are fairly well understood. It's the middle two stages, incubation and illumination, which remain the nub of the mystery.

Currently the tendency of neurophysiologists who have analyzed the latest cognitive-science research is to stress the relationship between knowledge and creativity. The unconscious does not regularly produce new ideas unless it has been conscientiously stuffed full of facts, impressions, and concepts. The unconscious, in order to weave its magic, must be given an assist through an endless series of conscious ruminations and attempted solutions. So face it, you'll have to make a major investment of time and effort before turning out really creative ideas. It means reading, listening, observing, mulling things over. Being truly creative requires that you grind up the grist of ideas with hard, disciplined work. It may be romantic to idle in a garret, hungry and apart from everyday concerns, waiting for inspiration to strike; but artistic temperament, as has been perceptively and chidingly put, is a luxury that only amateurs can afford.

The importance of knowledge and unremitting effort to creativity may better be appreciated when considering, among the many theories of how we go about giving birth to ideas, the following three distinct but related views.

Bisociation

Bisociation is Arthur Koestler's explanation of the creative process. He describes the act of creation as a linking or overlay of two or more thought matrices or frames of reference, which were previously unconnected with one another. Makes sense, right? We explore and probe among alternative frames, rather than just consciously focusing on one, until a fusion or synthesis takes place. Creativity is blocked, according to the bisociation theory, when there is a single-minded, narrowly focused concentration on but one matrix or frame of reference. Bisociation works best, in short, when the brain is not pushing on one level. Creativity thrives on spontaneity and free association. In such an open and accepting environment, an environment of play, additional matrices can bubble up around the original reference. Things can then start to connect, to fall into place. When everything connects, there is a feeling of euphoria and conquest.

Divergent and Convergent Thinking

Another theory of the creative process grew out of the research of Jacob Getzels, Philip Jackson, and Liam Hudson. As they see it, there are two sequential stages of processing information. The first stage is divergent thinking, the second convergent thinking. In the divergent stage, there is reformulation, elaboration, playing (there's that word again) with the problem as presented. This may include an outpouring of ideas, a kind of free association or brainstorming, to unblock thinking. Divergence may take place, and often does, unconsciously as the person is at sleep or rest. When there is a sense that the divergent thoughts have produced sufficient materials to solve a particular problem, then the process of converging upon precisely the right answer will begin.

As divergence is the making in the mind of many from one, convergence is the making of one from many. Creative persons will typically reformulate and elaborate the problem as presented, teasing out alternative possibilities. To the noncreative mind, the creative person may seem to be all over the lot, making bizarre, disconcerting, irrational leaps of thought. But at some point in the creative process, there is an intuitive feeling that the necessary ingredients of a new synthesis are now present. There is a calculated convergence upon a solution to the problem.

With a divergent and convergent creative process, order comes out of chaos, a plethora of possibilities are pruned to a few, diffuse ideas are brought into a sharp synthesis. All those haphazard neuron firings come together into a creative solution.

Lateral Thinking

A third, very workable way of harnessing the creative process concerns what is called lateral thinking, an approach to creativity described by Edward de Bono. Lateral thinking is very much a child of the right hemisphere, the intuitive, visual-spatial side of the brain. Its aim is to synthesize new patterns as it intuitively scans over known, stored patterns: bits and pieces searching for comfortable fits regardless of sequence.

Vertical thinking, the more usual step-by-step, logical mode of thinking, retains classes, categories, and labels and keeps everything buttoned up. Lateral thinking ignores the patterns and preconceptions and plays with different arrangements. Lateral thinking is very open and nonprejudicial. It does not shy away from exploring any alternative, regardless of whether it fit or worked earlier or not. Vertical thinking zeros in on the data with surgical precision, and if its assumptions hold up, it goes to the best logical alternative. Lateral thinking diverges and bisociates (to make a point on the relationship of the three theories), looking at the problem from multiple perspectives, looking for a better pattern.

In short, you could look at it this way: you'll never reach the summit of a peak previously climbed if you try to place your feet in exactly the same ridges and your fingers in exactly the same cracks as you did when you scaled the mount the first time.

The Bottom Line

Be it bisociation, divergent and convergent thinking, lateral thinking, or whatever, creativity is a spooky business. What we all have to remember is that however we get there, whichever thought process or processes are at work, eventually there comes a time when free-ranging thinking must cease and advertising deadlines must be met. As Oscar Wilde put it, "An ever-open mind is no better than an ever-open mouth."

6

On a Scale of One to Cerulean Blue, How Creative Are You?

A good spectator also creates.
—Swiss proverb

Right off let's get one thing straight—you are creative. Believe it and you'll achieve it. Creativity springs from a positive, make-it-happen attitude, not one that says "How do I fault me? Let me count the ways." When it's the bottom of the ninth, two outs, a man on base, and you're behind by a run, creativity is not thinking, "What if I strike out?" It's thinking, "Great! I'll hit it out of the park, win the game, and get lots of ink!"

It's being uninhibited. Accepting. It's being open to ideas, no matter how off-the-wall they may be. It's knowing that creativity is lurking in there somewhere, hunkered down behind all your defenses against looking foolish. It's understanding that creative people's ideas are like hothouse flowers. They need caressing and nurturing. They need to

Artwork structured by Christina Wong

bloom or at least bud before they're sent over to your mind's censorship lab to be dissected and magnified, turned inside out and upside down.

Where the Best Ideas Come From

Be encouraging to everyone with an idea, yourself included. Always remember that nobody has a corner on creativity. It comes in different sizes and shapes and infects the most humble and the most exalted.

For example, Tom Fuller, an illiterate black man who came to America as a slave when he was 14 years old, could give the exact number of seconds in any specified time period. When a gentleman celebrating his 70th birthday asked Tom how many seconds there had been thus far in his lifetime, Fuller turned it over in his mind for a moment and then correctly announced that the answer was 2,203,256,480. In England, it was an observant King George IV who decided that although shoes and boots were historically made to fit either foot, his boots would be designed specifically for each foot. So the well-shod George made the footwear industry what it is today. And that, too, was quite a feat.

Another thing to keep in mind, particularly if you don't have a Ph.D., is that although creativity is certainly enhanced by formal education, creativity does not depend on it. Four of the greatest American lawyers—Abraham Lincoln, Stephen A. Douglas, Daniel Webster, and John Marshall—never attended law school. In fact, Charles Dickens, Sean O'Casey, Noel Coward, Mark Twain, and Thomas Alva Edison never even graduated from grade school.

So no excuses. Whoever you are, you've got it.

Remember when you were a child? Remember that innate sense of wonder and curiosity: the pushing, pulling, piling up, taking apart that was part of nearly every waking moment? Remember the questions, the touching, the feeling, the looking around and under of anything and everything? You, me, all of us were born creative. In time we cover it up, put it under wraps. We deaden that joyous sensitivity, the experimentation and inventiveness that was part of our everyday life. So get rid of the wraps.

The Nature of Creativity

Creativity? It's a laugh, it's chocolate ice cream, it's a rainbow. It's built on a playful attitude. One of the great scientists at the turn of the century, Charles Steinmetz, would poke his head into the cubicles of the engineers and physicists hard at work on their projects in General Electric's research lab and ask, "Are you having any fun?" If there was no fun, there could be no breakthroughs.

Never, never think you are not creative. You are, to whatever degree, and can be even more so. If you believe this, you'll be comfortable and confident in judging creative work. This doesn't mean that all people are equally creative or that all people have the same kinds of creative bent. The flourishing neural garden of Einstein's brain was certainly more intricate and active than his housekeeper's. But if we may not be able to do much about the basic soil, we can very definitely do something about the fertilizing and tilling.

The one surefire way to improve upon the portion and quality of creativity that's been dished out to you is to regularly and vigorously use your mind. Exercise it. Stretch it. Study Italian if you agree, "Che idea!" If you hang in there for a year, you'll be able to speak and understand a basic vocabulary. Have some fun and start doing the crossword in *The New York Times* on Sundays. You may start off getting only a dozen or so entries, but in six months you'll finish it, in ink.

Whatever "stretching" exercises you choose, stick with them. Being creative may be fun, but it also takes work. X-rays of the Mona Lisa show that Leonardo made several different attempts at the portrait, each of the same woman, the wife of a Florentine merchant named

Francesco del Giocondo. They are all there, layered under the finished masterpiece as we know it today.

Such focused mental effort is not all that different from the activity used to develop a physical skill. If you've never played the piano, you can learn. You can take up gymnastics, ballet, or weight lifting and develop a level of skill and accomplishment in any of these fields that you wouldn't have imagined possible. You have to want to do it: you have to repeat and repeat, perfecting each fundamental. Finally you're doing it. Of course, you very likely won't be world-class, but you'll at least address the basics and better understand and appreciate the art and discipline of that particular skill.

Consider this. You're an executive. You have been in situations where you have had to persuade. Perhaps you came up through sales. You did well, or else you wouldn't have been promoted to your present position. What you said and how you said it often resulted in the action you wished to achieve. As you moved up the ranks, your performance, how you handled yourself, and the perceptions others had of you worked to your advantage in achieving specific goals. In every situation, both conscious and unconscious decisions were made on how to proceed. As often as not, these decisions had a creative aspect to them. As you succeeded, your creativity was demonstrated, in a variety of circumstances and through a variety of actions. The point is that you likely have already been using and exhibiting creativity, and that creativity isn't limited to a specific skill area. Thomas Alva Edison, who invented scores and scores of electric devices, also came up with wax paper.

Getting into a Creative Groove

Solving problems is partially an ability to look for patterns. For example, consider what this means:

MAN
BOARD

Once you've got it, other problems in the same genre become easy. When you've discovered that the stacked puzzle means *man overboard,* you'll easily know what these two mean:

STAND   WEAR
I   LONG

This will then lead to solving related problems, such as:

	R
HE'S/HIMSELF DEATH LIFE	ROAD
	A
	D

Some Creative Warm-Ups

The four puzzles below are classics. You've probably wrestled with all or most of them at one time or another. Maybe you've forgotten the answers. In any case, these stretching exercises should be a good way to get things started, as chances are you're most comfortable with logical, convergent, left-brain thinking that homes directly in on the correct solution. These puzzles are more related to this kind of cogitation. But there's enough right-brain action in the solving of all of these to make them a good place to start. You have to open up your mind and consider the possibilities. You have to apply some of that right-brain divergent, lateral thinking in coming around to the correct answer.

The riddle of the Sphinx

A granddaddy classic. The Sphinx, in Greek mythology, was a winged monster with the head of a woman and the body of a lion. It demanded that passersby answer a certain riddle and slew without mercy those who could not. But Oedipus solved the puzzle, whereupon the distraught Sphinx destroyed itself. The question: "What is it that walks on four legs in the morning, on two legs at noon, and on three legs in the evening?" OK, hang in there. Think it through for a moment before reading the answer. Think about what all those legs could mean. And don't necessarily take everything (like *morning, noon,* and *night*) literally.

Connecting the nine dots

This is another puzzle that has challenged us to think beyond the obvious. It demonstrates the power of opening your mind to a new approach when solving a problem. So again, think unconventionally, and be inventive and daring. Take a pencil, and connect all nine dots by drawing just four straight lines without lifting your pencil from the page.

Got it? Congratulations! You didn't restrict yourself to making connections from dot to dot within the boundaries of the square. You went beyond. If you didn't get it, don't worry. The answer is on the next page, and when you see it, you'll smile and say, "Of course!" Appreciating creativity is fundamental to being creative.

What time is it?

If it were two hours later, it would be half as long until noon as it would be if it were an hour later. What time is it?

What day is it?

The day before two days after the day before tomorrow is Wednesday. What day is today?

Answers:

The riddle of the Sphinx: A man. He crawls as a baby, walks upright as an adult, and uses a cane when elderly.

Connecting the nine dots:

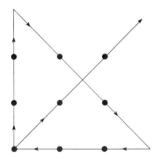

What time is it? 9:00 A.M.

What day is it? Tuesday.

These four warm-ups are, as noted earlier, essentially left-brain puzzles. The answers are relatively fixed and are arrived at mostly by convergent thinking.

The answer to this final warm-up is quite restricted by the given framework. It also is solved largely by putting convergent thinking to work. But this puzzle has more than one solution, and because of this, we do get a little farther into the Creative Zone.

Goat, Dog, and Cabbages

An Irish farmer needs to cross the Shannon River at a very narrow point near his home in Westmeath to take his young goat, his dog, and a few large, fresh cabbages to his sister's house in Roscommon. His boat is big enough to take him and either his goat, his dog, or the cabbages. The goat will surely eat the cabbages if left alone with them, and the goat will be eaten by the dog if the farmer leaves them alone. How did the farmer manage to ferry all three across safely?

Answer: There is more than one way to get the group together on the Roscommon shore all intact. For instance, the farmer could leave the cabbages and the dog and take the goat across. Then he would return and take the cabbages across but bring the goat back. He would next leave the goat and take the dog across. Then all he would have to do would be to go back and get the goat.

Test Your Creative I.Q.

Now that you're warmed up, try the following test of your creativity. It's not an examination that's been laboratory tested. There is no definitive measure that will determine that you are or are not creative. But you can score yourself and judge how ready you are for the Creative Zone.

So have fun! Open up your mind. Play around and take chances. Don't be afraid to stretch, to look foolish, and to be "wrong"—who will know anyway? Just answer all the questions you can. And keep in mind, appreciating the answer is about as important as getting it "right." The main thing is to think creatively and keep stretching your mind.

1. Here's a challenge I put to some guests at a dinner party in
    New York. See if you can put together a logical explanation for
    the following conversation:
    "I'm going to be meeting with the curator of Twentieth
    Century Art at the Metropolitan Museum of Art the day after
    tomorrow."
    "Oh, that's wonderful. Could you do me an enormous favor
    and drop off a small Grecian urn at the Boston Museum of Fine
    Arts?"
    It is an enormous advantage for anyone charged with
    developing or approving creativity to be able to think in terms
    of semiotics, a philosophical theory that is concerned in part
    with understanding the meanings and nuances in signs,
    symbols, and situations. In the case of the above dialogue, it
    may seem somewhat Kafkaesque if you assume, as most
    people at the dinner party did, that the reported conversation
    took place in New York. However, think of the words again
    when I tell you that the conversation took place in Sydney,
    Australia.
    Score 10 points if you saw that a geographic shift gave a
    totally different dimension to the conversation.

2. Look at the two shapes below. One is called *Tickatee*. The other
    is called *Mumbawama*. Which is which?

    Right! Tickatee is the one on the left. Which, naturally,
    leaves us with Mumbawama on the right. Really there is no
    correct answer. Either shape could have either name. However,
    for the great majority of people, the name *Tickatee* feels right

for the hard, angular shape, and *Mumbawama* has a warm, sensuous sound, compatible with the billowing shape.

We are interested in creativity that persuades. In advertising we want to strike a responsive chord with as many individuals in the target market as we can. We want to build bridges that will lead to sales. We are not looking to be discordant, out of synch, outlandish, uncomfortably pushy and challenging, or irritating. We want to establish a comfort level with our prospects. We want to make friends.

Score 5 points if you felt *Tickatee* was the name more suited to the angular shape.

3. Make up a little drama based on the reality of your office. Use the characters around you. Keep them as they are, or change them slightly to add drama. Confine it to just a page. Need help starting? OK: "Once upon a time . . ." Only kidding. You can come up with a more creative opening than that! (10 minutes)

Score 5 points if the story pretty much reflects reality. Score 10 points if you added characters, stretched the truth, or even injected some fantasy or ingenious plot turns. If you didn't do any of these things, write it again, and do some of these things. Then give yourself 10 points.

4. Make up names from words or simple phrases. A few starters:

    Jim Nasium
    Mary Goround
    Ben Dover
    Ed Youkayshun
    Ella Cueshun
    (Three minutes)

Take 1 point for every name you added. But sharpen your creative judgment by being pretty hard-nosed about the names you accept. Don't buy a real stretch. You say you had 10 good ones? Shirley Ujest.

5. Everyone groans in mock agony (or maybe real agony) whenever punned upon. But punning is a creative, playful exercise.

Try giving some fresh, if twisted, meanings to any 10 words you choose. For instance:

bulldoze—Ferdinand is sleeping
jargon—the glass container is missing
overtired—a car with five wheels
bigamist—a thicker fog

Score 1 point for every definition that really works. You be the judge.

6. Punctuate this so it makes sense.

time flies I cant theyre too fast

Remember to look beyond the obvious. Try making *flies* a noun. Toss it around for 30 seconds (get out your stopwatch) before reading the answer below.

Time flies? I can't. They're too fast.

Score 5 points if you figured out that you had been asked to find out how fast flies fly.

7. Let's see how fast those synapses fire. In just 30 seconds, write down 10 words beginning with the letters *ga*. Then write down 10 words with the letters *ga* within the word. Examples: *gasp* and *subjugate*.

Score 1 point for every word you got within the allotted time.

8. List as many different ways as you can think of in five minutes to use a bucket and one other object. Examples: a shade for a lamp, a pedestal for a sculpture.
    Score 1 point for every combination you came up with.

9. Describe each word listed below with a rhyming word (or words). Example: wine/fine wine.

    rain
    fight
    Annabelle
    yellow
    bunny
    daisy
    pony
    class
    weights
    letter

    Score 1 point for every combination that works without strain.

10. Finish the limerick.

    There once was a writer most clever
    Whose ads Starched higher than ever
    Dah dah dah dah dah dah
    Dah dah dah dah dah dah
    Dah dah dah dah dah dah dah dever

Score 10 if it scans right and is funny (dirty or not). Take off as many points as you think appropriate if it doesn't and isn't.

Now add up your score. A total of 50 points is excellent. If you scored that much, or nearly that much, you probably rank high on the Lifetime Creativity Scale (see below), and you're well on your way into the Creative Zone.

The Lifetime Creativity Scale

Dr. Ruth Richards, a psychiatrist, and Dr. Dennis Kinney, a psychologist, both of the Harvard Medical School, developed a measure of creativity that they call the Lifetime Creativity Scale. Their findings, based on a structured interview with some 461 men and women, indicate that fewer than one percent have so-called exceptional creativity. About 10 percent can be considered high in creativity, and a full 60 percent can be described as having moderate creativity.

The Bottom Line

Take heart. Just by virtue of your interest in reading this book, you are quite likely to be one of those 60 percent who have at least some capacity for creativity. A representative of the lower level of creativity, the bottom 30 percent, would likely have a life-style given over to prescribed routines. An example offered by Drs. Richards and Kinney is that of a bricklayer who after 20 years of work inherited a substantive trust fund and immediately retired to spend most of the rest of his waking hours watching television.

What is creativity? As Louis Armstrong said when asked what jazz is, "Man, if you gotta ask you'll never know." So hone your own personal capacity for creativity to a sharp point. Just feel it. And appreciate it when it's right in front of your nose.

7

The Secret Of Living In
The Creative Zone

To approve is more difficult than to admire.
—Hofmannsthal

There is a psychological state known as *hypomania*. When possessed by it, one feels a slightly or even markedly high level of elation and hyperactivity. It is a mania to be devoutly desired. If you haven't had it, catch it. If you've got it, spread it around and hope that it becomes epidemic. Hypomania is a flush of increased energy and self-confidence, when more and better ideas emerge. When you feel it, ride with it, challenge the status quo, take some risks. Risks are what you must take if you are going to be truly creative.

In creating an atmosphere in which creativity can flourish, for yourself and for others, it is essential that you avoid being negative. Granted, you have to draw the line, set up parameters, and reject those things that are clearly destructive and off the mark. Your advertising must not equivocate or be untruthful. It must not offend or be inconsistent with your company's basic corporate culture. If what is presented to you for approval has any of these characteristics, you have every right to glower, pound the table, and say no. That is not being negative.

Keep in mind that there is a very strong element of play in creativity. It allows the childlike facets of our characters and personalities to come forth and glitter. So when evaluating someone else's creative effort, remember a basic principle of child psychology—praise works better than punishment.

75

Three Roadblocks to Creative Evaluation

To most effectively nurture creativity you have to be very careful to avoid three major pitfalls:

Premature evaluation: Too many supervisory executives inhibit creativity by screening and judging an idea prematurely. An old name for a ball of thread is a *clue.* That's the reason we say it's necessary to unravel the clues to solve a mystery. Like a ball of thread, creative clues must be carefully unraveled in order to reach the center of the idea. So keep your mind open, and don't be too judgmental in the early part of the process.

Constant surveillance: Over-the-shoulder monitoring interrupts the rhythm of creative development. There is a simmering period, a time of incubation that is necessary for generating ideas. A part of this process (as you'll remember from chapter 5) is subconscious. Give it time to happen. Interrupting the process sets the journey to a truly creative solution back. It provokes people into shifting too soon into conscious effort, which inevitably means a less original, more imitative and backward-looking solution.

Excessive competition: Pitting group against group, team against team can also brutalize creativity. It introduces an anxiety that forces the issue and, like premature evaluation and constant surveillance, channels thinking into replaying previously approved ideas. Competition can work to an advantage if manipulated with skill, but superior talents are driven by their own need for perfection and can be put off by a contest whose judges they don't necessarily trust.

These, and related conditions, make people prefer the safest option. They make people pull back from trying riskier and therefore possibly more creative, possibilities.

Insisting on Creativity

But, you say, if I don't keep prodding, pushing, and kicking, I don't get any action from my agency. If that's the case, here's some advice: fire them.

You must have copywriters, art directors, and marketing people who are driven to solve problems if you really want sizzling creativity. You must have people who honestly and passionately care, who find that making extraordinary ads is the most exciting thing they could be doing. They may not be easy to find, but they're out there; light the lamp and play Diogenes. If you do, you may find chapter 10 illuminating.

Just what is and what isn't creative is not easily defined. For one thing, a creative solution is seldom if ever something completely different. Please note well that creative advertising almost always consists of new arrangements of old ideas. The truth is, as one old sage put it, "There's not a thought in our head which hasn't been worn shiny in other heads." When it comes to crafting a creative ad, ideas have to be rearranged, and there is no single correct solution. If there were, we would have the one perfect ad for a given product, and no new ads would ever be needed. And, no new ads, with no fresh angles, twists, combinations, or permutations, would make for very dull, boring, and ineffective advertising. The fact is that there are many rearrangements of old ideas that are fresh, creative, and highly effective. At the same time, there are literally millions of ineffective, absolutely wrong ways to go. The trick is to know which are which.

Creativity and Focusing

The creative life begins when you focus on purpose. What are you trying to get across? What do you want to happen? It begins when you shake down your calloused, long-accumulated defenses. Get rid of preconceived concepts. Get rid of extraneous information, and get to the heart of the matter.

For example, zero in on the important information in this puzzle: A pet falcon is flying 60 miles an hour between two boys. Jack is on a 24-inch mountain bike, and Zack is on a 28-inch, ten-speed racing bike. They are pedaling toward each other at 10 miles an hour. When the falcon reaches one boy, it wheels around and flies back toward the other, repeating this until Jack and Zack meet in 30 minutes. How far has the falcon flown in that time?

Forget all the stuff about boys named Jack and Zack, mountain bikes and racing bikes, 10 miles an hour, and back and forth. The falcon has flown for 30 minutes at 60 miles an hour; so, it has covered 30 miles. Don't complicate things. As Spencer Tracy put it when describing acting, "Just learn your lines and don't bump into the furniture."

Putting Heuristic Reasoning to Work

The heuristic (experimental) approach to solving problems goes back to the days of Euclid. It was pursued later by Descartes, Leibniz, and the less-familiar Bernhard Bolzano. The aim of the technique was to study the method and rules of discovery and invention. If we know the process and can control it, we will get to the solution more certainly.

What we're exploring here, in regard to advertising, has been going on for centuries and centuries, especially in the discipline of mathematics. But it can be very useful for you to be aware of and to practice heuristic reasoning when creating advertising. You may not be a copywriter or an art director, but like it or not, by participating in the approval process of advertising, you are very much participating in the creative process. You're either a filter and collaborator or a bottleneck and roadblock.

It is important to keep in mind that heuristic reasoning does not give complete certainty. In solving a difficult mathematical problem, for example, heuristic reasoning is employed by taking educated guesses and following plausible solution routes. Eventually what is sought, in this mathematical instance, is rigorous proof. But heuristic reasoning is not the end of the journey, just the road to getting there.

In advertising there is no such thing as a final, positive solution, so don't look for it. There are, of course, lots of satisfactory answers to an advertising need—and legions upon legions of bad ones. Heuristic reasoning is an open-minded process that can help you arrive at one or more of those few action-provoking ideas that we're pursuing.

Why Creativity Is a Must

Seventy percent of all TV commercials are ignored. Of the 30 percent that win attention, about 80 percent are misunderstood.

Only 22 percent of all radio commercials succeed in communicating their message.

Only one out of four print ads manage to communicate any positive message for a product. More than 65 percent of the ads in a magazine are forgotten after four minutes.

Five years ago there were some 10,000 different products and brands on a supermarket's shelves. Today there are over 18,000. Last year more than 3,400 new products were introduced to the American market. At least 80 percent won't make it and will be taken off the shelves within 24 months.

These findings (from research conducted by the Pretesting Company, Englewood, New Jersey) underline why relevant, action-provoking creativity is essential.

The Bottom Line

In promoting any product today, whether fashions or automobiles or die-stamping machines or insurance policies, the competition for attention is a never-ending, sisyphean task. Every advantage you can wring out of your advertising approach can make a difference of hundreds and hundreds of thousands of dollars in sales. So let's start wringing.

8
Creativity In Print

Handle your tools without mittens.
—Benjamin Franklin

How do we know if something is really going to work? Well, we've got past experience to help us, but no one can reduce successful advertising to a formula. What works and why, and what doesn't work and why not has been researched, philosophized about, pontificated upon, and argued over ever since Eve persuaded Adam that she knew how to keep the doctor out of the Garden of Eden.

Thinking about and intelligently using the principles discussed in this book can assure you of a good ad or commercial. Enormously effective, action-provoking creativity can't be guaranteed. But if you aim for it, at least you'll get good, do-the-job, worth-the-money advertising. Even Babe Ruth didn't hit a home run every time he stepped up to the plate: what we want to avoid is that all to common advertising that doesn't work hard enough to justify the budget applied to it.

Approving a Billboard

A billboard is to understanding advertising what the Dick and Jane primer is to understanding reading. The fundamental lesson in creating successful advertising, which we can learn most dramatically from billboards, is the necessity of conveying a positive idea in a fleeting moment, while unmistakably identifying your company or product with that idea. If you don't do both these things, whether with a billboard, a magazine spread, or a 30-second TV commercial, you've spent a lot of money for nothing.

81

Three things to look for

Here are the ABCs of billboard effectiveness, the principles of which apply to all advertising.

1.   The driver of an automobile moving along at 45 miles an hour can barely read nine words of copy. That's half as many words as are in the preceding sentence. And hoping that someone can comprehend those nine words is really stretching your expectations. It's better for you to have but five or six words on any sign adjacent to a major roadway.

2.   The ability of a viewer to handle a given number of words depends on several factors, including the number and makeup of the visual elements. A relatively complex visual with multiple points of interest would allow only a few words to register. A simpler visual allows for the possibility of including more words.

3.   A bold visual and a clever, memorable message means nothing if they don't connect to the product. Nearly one-third of all those billboards that test very well for communicating a strong message or slogan generate poor advertiser identification among viewers. This means that one out of three of the best ones, those registering a strong message or slogan, turn out to be absolutely worthless! Don't blame the outdoor advertising people. They just provide the white space. It's up to you to use it effectively to make your point.

Let me give two specially created examples of what doesn't and what does work. Both are presented in rough comp form.

CHICAGO IS OUR KIND OF TOWN

THAT'S WHY WE FLY THERE EVERY HOUR 8 AM TO 8 PM.

EAGLE AIRLINES

Pretty good, right? The head uses a pluralization of the key line from the well-known unofficial theme song of Chicago. This might be a very legitimate approach if it were concurrently being used on radio and TV, as all would tie together. Some of the best campaigns have been those that cross-fertilize and compound the message by building one medium upon the other. With any kind of advertising weight on broadcasting, the song would register with a significant number of people, and when one of those people saw the billboard, they would "hear" the song, giving the board more impact and dimension. However, the weaknesses in this particular prototype approach are (1) too many words, (2) a generic photo of Chicago that visually says no more than the word *Chicago* in the head, and (3) a too-small advertiser name.

EAGLE™ TO CHICAGO.
EVERY HOUR 8AM TO 8PM.

EAGLE AIRLINES

Cloud Streak Aerobus

Comps by Bob Fudge

Compare the two boards. Imagine them in context; that is, put yourself in the shoes of the driver of a car passing each. Those things that give the second its impact and memorability are (1) all the necessary information presented in just eight words (fewer are desirable, but in this case "8am to 8pm" essentially reads as a unit); (2) a bold, simple visual that focuses on the product; and (3) two very strong advertiser identifications, one in the headline, the other in the visual.

In advertising what is creative is that which helps a good premise work better. Creative can be being ingenious with a play on words; it can be being shocking; it can be being outrageous. It can be any and all these things and more. Most importantly it can be simple, unadorned, and direct. Don't ignore the former, but look first for the latter. It's the place to start and often the place to stop.

Let's assume, in this hypothetical situation, that the fictitious Eagle Airline has other flights from various airports. The second board we created could be made to work anywhere by changing the city name and flight time information, depending on the frequency of flights from the specific city. There is no need to say, for instance, "Atlanta to Chicago." The board appearing in Atlanta will be assumed to mean *from Atlanta,* as those in Kansas City will be assumed to mean *from Kansas City.* One of the creative elements of the solution is economy of production, as well as economy of elements. Essentially the same board can be used in multiple marketing situations by simply altering the second line.

Consider the visual of the aircraft itself. Obviously, if the airline features new, short-range CloudStreak Aerobuses, the visual should be of a CloudStreak Aerobus. Some sophisticated fliers will notice, and if the CloudStreak is hot, Eagle scores more points. We may even put a bold caption by the plane, *CloudStreak Aerobus.* More importantly we decided to use a very gutsy, efficient-looking painting of the plane to emphasize strength and reliability to the frequent business traveler. The plane turns into speed lines on the left side of the poster, visually suggesting fast, efficient, no-nonsense, on-time service.

The point is that creativity is not always found on a large scale, although that is certainly where it's most evident. Don't forget that a significant part of creativity is in small details.

So when it comes to billboards, start with the basics:

1. Use large type.

2. Don't place your key message over a visual so that the message is harder to read.

3. Remember that product visuals are better than generic visuals.

4. Use five words or less.

5. Boldly show the label or brand name.

6. Keep layouts, colors, and key messages consistent with all your other advertising.

7. Consider how the board would look in different situations. (Would a basically green background be lost on a board positioned in front of green trees? Would the design and colors work against both a cloudy, hazy sky and a blue sky?)

These are good, solid fundamentals to consider in reviewing any form of advertising. Just adapt point 7: consider the editorial and advertising environment in print, and consider the programming, time slot, and competitive environment in broadcasting. And, although you should observe these fundamentals, keep your mind open, and be ready to make exceptions and take reasonable chances.

If it ain't broke don't fix it.

Keep it simple. A few words. A bold, connecting visual. To make the point, Bob Kwait, the creative director of Philips-Ramsey, put tongue in cheek and prepared this visual sequence for use by the Institute of Outdoor Advertising. The first treatment is fun and makes the point in one visual bite. From number 2 on the plot thickens and impact is progressively lost.

Billboard Ads That Work

There are no mysteries with billboards. To sum up the secret to success in creating billboards that work, "Let it all hang out." Say it short
and sweet and don't stint on the size of your logo. The following
Obie Award winners are examples of billboards "that work."

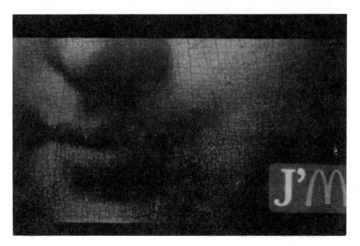

These two billboards, both Obie Award winners from the Institute of Outdoor Advertising, take simplicity to the limit. Because Nissan (created by Chiat/Day/Mojo) and McDonald's (created by Cossette Communication Marketing) are very visible, well known advertisers, the simplicity speaks volumes.

Seabrook presents problem (visually) and solution (verbally). A wonderful, efficient use of words playing off picture (created by Thompson & Co.). Levi's double entendre (created by Harrod & Mirlin) suggests that therein lies a tale. A novel or a soap opera? The viewer can bring to it what they will. Two more Obie Award winners.

A pun is fun. And so is music and a good time out with friends. J&B's Obie Award winner (created by Grace and Rothschild) uses its label colors to insure product identification. The Club Med Obie Award billboard (created by Ammirati & Puris) positioned in and around busy, trafficky areas makes its which-would-you-prefer point.

Approving a Magazine or Newspaper Ad

The first duty of a print ad is to get itself read. If an ad isn't read, then no matter how extraordinary the information or clever the words, nothing is going to happen. And if the ad is read, it doesn't mean a thing if it doesn't cause the name of the product to register in the prospect's mind. That's obvious, right? Well, if it's so obvious, the question to be answered is, Why do so many print ads fail to accomplish these two musts?

In looking at a proposed magazine or newspaper ad, remember to get into the shoes of the person you're trying to reach. Think like the prospect, not like the boss. This is not easy. You know the walls at the office are a light gray, there's green carpeting in the halls, J.C. founded the company and still is most comfortable doing things the way he did five, six, seven years ago, when sales went through the roof. The prospect knows none of this, and cares less. You've got to wipe clean as much as you can of all the minutiae and even the corporate culture that distinguishes your company (there's plenty of time later on to see that the ad is in accord with the character of the firm) and consider how the proposed ad will influence the prospect.

Here's a trick. Pretend that the ad was created by your principal competitor. Hold it at arm's length, and take a quick look at it. Do you get it? Is there something in the combination of the headline and the visual that catches your attention? Can you easily identify the product or the company name? Do you wish it was your ad, rather than theirs? Be as dispassionate as you can in this test.

Typography

There are a few important points to remember when considering typography:

1. Small type is difficult to read and, more often than not, won't get read.

2. Very large type can be as hard to read as very small type.

3. Reverse type, such as white type on a black or dark background, is more difficult to read than black type on a white

background. Reverse type can be used effectively, but it must be against an even background, and the type might well have to be larger than if it were on a plain white background.

Some typefaces read better than others. Resist getting too outlandish with type. Stay in character with the mood of the ad, but go for readability above all else. Be aware that uppercase-and-lowercase usually (but not always) reads better than all-caps. This is influenced by a number of things, including the size and character of the type used and the number of words.

Type on a page has a "color" and shape within the space that should be in harmony with the tone and intent of the message. A conservative typeface (one that is commonly seen and doesn't draw attention to itself), used to present a relatively small headline followed by very evenly placed text (somewhat like paragraphs in a book or magazine) might work effectively for a serious, quality-oriented announcement. On the other hand, bold, jaunty type, perhaps even at contrasting angles, could suggest fun and excitement and might be suitable in an advertisement for, say, a rock concert or an opening. The "attitude" of the type, the "sound" that it suggests, can work with the message to communicate both the essentials of what you want to say and the mood and feeling of the subject.

Making decisions on the typeface; the size of the type used for the headline, for text, and for crossheads; whether to use underlines or italics; the spacing between elements; the amount of white space on all sides; and other points both obvious and subtle takes considerable skill on the part of the art director and dramatically impacts the personality, appeal, and effectiveness of any ad—all-type or very little type.

Layout

Simplicity is the cardinal virtue. Complicated, unfocused layouts do not get the same kind of attention and readership as simple, direct layouts that come right to the point. This does not mean that a layout with considerable copy and a number of visual elements can't win high attention and readership: simplicity is not limited to a big photo and a few words. The key to a strong, compelling layout is that there must be a central focus. There must be some element—a photograph, an illustration, the headline—that wins attention and involves the prospect with one or more of the other elements. Do first things first. Gain attention, make a point, even a superficial one, and register who you are. If you do this much, you have created some awareness among your prospects. Of course, if you can get that far, there is a good chance that considerable numbers of the prospects will take the next step and actually become involved with the ad, thus reinforcing the message and allowing it to be thoroughly comprehended.

The visual

Photography is, unsurprisingly, the most frequently used medium for the visuals of advertisements. A photograph is closer to reality than an illustration. There is more believability with a photograph, less of a question of faking it.

The visual, whether a photograph or an illustration, must connect to the premise of the copy. If you are discussing the seaworthiness and sleek design of a new cabin cruiser, a photograph of a softball player, swinging at a pitch and wearing a team sponsor's shirt that reads, "Pizza De Resistance," doesn't forward the selling message. A beautiful mermaid coupled with a headline that reads, "Fantasy Becomes Reality," might work considerably better. After all, mermaids are thought to be sleek, beautiful, and very seaworthy. And the headline suggests a breakthrough in developing the ideal cruiser. But there had better be a good photo of the boat, as well as Miss Wet-and-Wonderful, even if it is a smaller image in an inset.

A bold, simple photograph has more power than a complicated, multisubject photo. This too, like so many suggestions and observations, has exceptions (remember, we're avoiding rules). You'll be better off, however, if you can make your point and visually connect to the creative concept with a focused, very direct, minimal photograph, rather than with a complex picture that has several focal points.

Showing the product itself, treating it as the "hero," is a surefire way to achieve simplicity and the strongest kind of brand identification. The danger is that if everyone just showed their product and said, in effect, "Here it is!" we'd have uninspired, uncaptivating, dull, boring advertising. It is essential to have a creative twist, whether it be a clever few words or the simple addition of a prop appearing with the product.

Photographs of people are among the strongest visuals of all. Research studies over the years have shown that a head shot with eye contact consistently gets top attention. But here again, as with almost every element in the process of crafting an ad, it depends on how it's done. The casting must be appropriate to the product or concept. The verbal-visual connection must be good. The quality and nature of the photograph, the size in proportion to the type, the freshness in how these elements are arranged are all critical to making something a hit, not a near miss.

For an example of the effectiveness of images of people, we can examine photography in travel advertising. Such advertising is very compelling. It shows an (idealized) view of what the place looks like; you've seen the gorgeous photographs of Norwegian fjords, ancient Irish castles, beaches in the Virgin Islands, giraffes on African savannas, or landmarks such as Notre-Dame and London's Tower Bridge. Depending on the point of view of the ad, photos of places can be stronger when people are in them. A photo of a canal in Venice is not as enticing or romantic as one that includes a couple in a gondola. And sometimes even a close-up of a person that shows little of the specific location itself can evoke very strong mental images and be especially appealing.

Although in more cases than not a photograph is a stronger, more effective visual than an illustration, there are exceptions. The style and quality of the art and its appropriateness to the concept is as difficult to deal with in illustration, maybe more so, than in photography. If the all-time great recruitment poster of Uncle Sam pointing and saying, "I WANT YOU," had been created by Picasso in his cubist period, it would not have been as effective as the classic created by James Montgomery Flagg. In using illustration, many of the same caveats that we've discussed throughout this chapter apply. Keep it simple and keep it relevant. The style and character of the art must be totally compatible with the creative concept of the ad and, of course, the product and company.

Illustration works particularly well in depicting a product that is not yet a reality. A new real estate development may use an illustration to show what the building will look like when finished, or a pharmaceutical advertisement may use a cutaway illustration of the circulatory system to make clear a point about the medication and how it will work.

Concept

Type, photography, and illustration are all very important. But the most critical element of the ad is its concept. In judging an ad, the first question to be answered is, "What's the creative character of the ad, its concept, that makes it different, fresh, a reason for the reader to attend?"

Concept can be defined in any number of ways. It is the essential "story" of an ad. It is the hook, the point of view, the basic positioning of the message. The following are six examples of concepts that not only worked at their first appearance (which is all you can really ask of an advertisement) but have held up over time as well.

I created this poster to counteract the image of Ireland as—rural, quaint, and less urbane than it actually is. The poster has won scores of awards and prompted dozens and dozens of imitators.

I wrote this newspaper ad to portray *Business Week* as being able to offer advertisers longer life than could one of its most formidable competitors. This was named the best newspaper business ad the year it appeared.

The commission was to create an ad for *Vogue* that would sell the virtues of Italian furs; but because there were over 30 designers involved, no furs were to be shown. The solution was to make a connection between the sensitivity to and understanding of the female body shown by Michelangelo, Botticelli, and other Italian masters and the similar artistry of today's Italian fur designers. The ad generated a strong response and won a Creativity of the Year Award.

The biggest, most expensive TV syndication in history was that
of "The Cosby Show." I created this ad, one in a series, to urge TV
executives who aspired to have their stations be number one in
their communities to have the courage to invest in the show. The
result was an enormously successful sales effort, the most syndication dollars of all time.

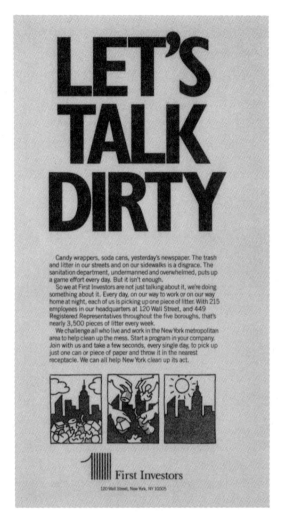

I wrote this full-page newspaper ad for a financial company, First Investors. They had organized their own employees and a great many other major New York City corporations in an effort to help clean up the litter on New York's streets. David Grayson, their president, coined the slogan we put on all participants' buttons, "NY is picking up."

This was one of a series of ads I created for *The Economist.* The copy in this ad suggests that the information in each weekly issue is so hot and stimulating to its devoted readers that they'd be happy if their subscription copies came in a plain brown wrapper.

Two final points: even if you do everything right and are inspired, ingenious, and altogether brilliant, the whole thing is wasted if no one knows who's running the ad. Nearly half of all ads present a brand name or company logo that does not have enough presence. Let's see it. And if the concept calls for it, don't worry where you put it: at the top, in the middle, or down in the right-hand corner, where it usually ends up.

Creativity doesn't stop with the right concept, words, layout, models, color, and so forth. All these things have to work with each other, a variety of components coming together in the right place. It's no different from real life. A lovely woman in an Adolfo gown, wearing diamonds and emeralds, with her hair beautifully coiffed and her makeup exquisitely and intelligently applied, will fit in better at a black-tie benefit in the Rainbow Room than at an appendectomy in the operating room. Although in advertising there is something to be said for getting attention with the unexpected, there has to be a reason, a connection to the product.

Placement

Once you are satisfied that you have a creative, hardworking ad, don't think that it's all over. David Lean's *Lawrence of Arabia* does not work on a 13-inch TV in the same way that it works on the big screen in a movie theater. The creative product with which you and your agency have taken such pains must likewise be shown off in the right environment to maximize its advantage. A sizzling creative product will work virtually anywhere, and the most important component in advertising is a strong, intelligently realized creative concept; but any ad can work harder if you keep several further points in mind.

Your first concern should be with the strength of the ad, not where in the publication it's placed. The stronger an ad, the less the concern about the advertising or editorial environment. An exceptionally strong ad will usually perform well no matter where it is placed. Despite conventional wisdom, there is evidence that right-hand pages and left-hand pages in magazines and newspapers work equally well.

Don't be too concerned about the front of the book versus the back of the book. Forty percent of all readers do not start at the front of the book. They fan the pages with their left hand and look at ads and articles back to front. As a matter of fact, years ago the most-read section of *Time* magazine was "People," which appeared toward the back of each issue. That fact inspired Time Inc. to start *People Weekly* magazine, built on the concept of that section, and today *People* sells over three million copies a week.

An ad in a large-magazine format will score no better than the same ad in a small-magazine format (such as *Reader's Digest* or *TV Guide*). Likewise, a tabloid is as effective as a large-size newspaper.

Spread ads do not on average generate over 12 percent more brand name recall than a single-page ad. There are times, depending on marketing concerns, when the spread arrangement can justify the doubled cost. In fact, multiple-page ads may well be worth the price, as the second or third page (if the creative concept is sound and well executed) might well catch a reader's attention and be intriguing enough to direct his or her attention back to the first page.

Freestanding inserts

Create the insert with basic rules of print advertising in mind. Don't consider FSIs as merely a discount or a special offer. Tell the reader why he or she should be interested in the product in the first place. Point out your advantages and your competitive differences. Then clinch the sale with the coupon offer.

CAUTION:
Be aware that a significant discount can hurt the prestige of an upscale or unique product. Your offer should not be the same as or too much like offers of similar brands that have less exclusive images. Tying in with an inappropriate service or other brand can also seriously damage the image of your product.

Newspaper Ads that Work

One measure of advertising that works in newspapers is what the Newspaper Advertising Association thinks works. Their annual Cerative Newspaper awards issue is a selection of the best in large space, small space, black-and-white, and color with an Athena awarded to the best in its category.

Timberland

Timberland. Where the elements of design are the elements themselves.

Unlike other footwear makers, who slavishly follow the winds of change, we Timberland people take our inspiration from the winds that never change. Be they the mighty gales that loosen the Carolina coast, the sandstorms that parch the Southwestern canyons, or the tropical sea mists that dance across the Pacific, calling you to points unknown.

It has always been our belief that the elements that shape the earth itself, the very ground we walk on, should also shape the shoes in which we walk. Whether our path leads to the highest peak in Colorado or the tallest skyscraper in Chicago.

And whether we are from the West or East. Western or men. These elements, quite simply, are wind, water, earth and sky. In alliance with the world's most enduring leathers, they are the elements that make up our entire women's collection. Designed for today. And years from today.

Boots, shoes, clothing, wind, water, earth and sky.

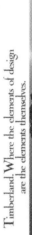

Smith & Wolensky

Positioning, the marketing process followed in order to have a product perceived in a specific way, is very strongly at work here. Smith & Wolensky's headline claims the position of one of the six best steak houses in the world (created by Angotti, Thomas, Hedge, Inc.).

Illinois

Looks like the fish are biting in Illinois.

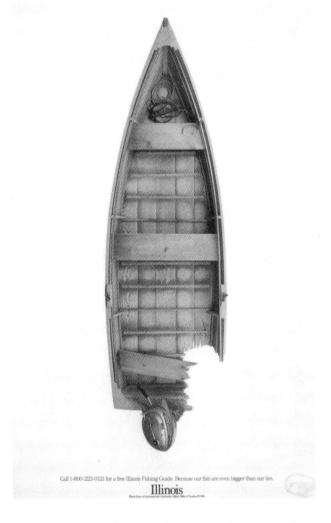

Call 1-800-223-0121 for a free Illinois Fishing Guide. Because our fish are even bigger than our lies.

Illinois

The ad for the Illinois Office of Tourism (created by Zechman And Associates) visually tells the kind of fish story that fisherman want to believe. Dramatic, fun, and with right-to-the-point copy.

Dos Locos

MEXICAN FOOD SO AUTHENTIC YOU'LL THINK TWICE BEFORE DRINKING THE WATER.

Dos Locos   92 Exchange Street, Portland, ME 04101,
Phone 77-LOCOS   Open 7 Days a Week.

When it comes to dining in Mexico everyone knows that the slaking of one's thirst can be a flirtation with catastrophe. Dos Locos may be a couple of crazies but they know how to shrewdly make a point (created by Jim & Dan).

Utah Symphony, WCEZ

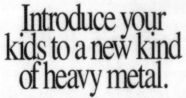

Introduce your kids to a new kind of heavy metal.

Conduct this simple test. If your kids recognize Poison over Paganini, Ratt over Ravel or Bon Jovi over Beethoven, introduce them to the metal heads at Symphony Hall, performing live classical concerts for kids of all ages.

This season's Youth Series concerts feature a colorful tour through America and Russia with the BYU Folk Dancers, a musical treasure hunt combining mime and magic, and the unique dances of the Ririe-Woodbury Dance Company.

Expose your children to musical experiences that will enrich their lives long after the latest sound has passed. Season tickets are $10 for adults, $5 for children and only $24 for the entire family.

October 22, the Utah Symphony and the BYU Folk Dancers. Symphony Hall, 10:00 a.m. or 11:30 a.m. Tickets $2 for children, $4 for adults. (No babes in arms, please.) Utah Symphony Box Office: 533-6407.

UTAH SYMPHONY

"We tried playing other radio stations at the office, but the ferns died."

In offices all over Columbia, people are discovering that beautiful music from WCEZ both powers to make plants grow and charms to soothe the savage beas.

WCEZ
FM Stereo 93.5 / The Beautiful Place To Be

Rap and rock may be the music that fills stadiums and floods the airwaves but both classical and beautiful music will have their day. The Utah Symphony ad (created by Williams & Rockwood) offers a civilized alternative with a clever play on heavy metal, while WCEZ uses outrageous exaggeration and variations on a couple of common expressions in its ad (created by Harper Hellams & Paige) to help bring sanity back to the aural environment.

Montclair

When Kids Plan To Commit Suicide, They Usually Tell You First.

They tell you in little ways. Maybe not with words, but actions. And when they do, you need to get them help. Fast.

But fortunately, most kids show signs of depression long before they become suicidal.

That's when you can help most.

First, understand that depression, though very serious, is very common. Especially in the difficult teenage years.

But most important, learn to recognize the symptoms.

Is your child constantly tired? Has he or she substantially lost or gained weight? Is he or she irritable, restless or unable to concentrate? Does your child generally feel sad, hopeless, worthless or guilty? Is your child having too many behavioral problems at school?

Depression is usually triggered when a loss is suffered. (It can also be triggered by a chemical imbalance in the brain.) Has a loved one died recently? Has there been a divorce or separation in your family? Has your child experienced a breakup with a serious boyfriend

"Clean house" by giving away favorite possessions, cleaning his or her room or throwing things away.

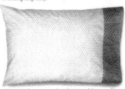
A change in sleep patterns such as sleeping much later or waking up two hours earlier than usual, taking a lot of naps or not sleeping well.

Abuse of alcohol or drugs, accompanied by red eyes, dilated pupils, slurred speech.

Thoughts of death or suicide with comments such as "I'd be better off dead" or "Nothing matters, it's no use."

or girlfriend? Is there a drug or alcohol problem in the family?

Granted, all kids go through "phases" or bouts of depression. But when several of the symptoms occur for longer than a few weeks, it's not a phase.

It's a serious illness that needs treatment.

Fortunately, great strides have been made in the treatment of depression. It is the easiest of all behavioral problems to treat. And that's what we're here to do. Through therapy and/or medication, we can work with your child on developing greater self-esteem and becoming better adjusted.

For more information call the Behavioral Medicine Center at Baptist Montclair at 877-8700 or toll-free 1-800-421-2065.

And listen to your kid with your eyes as well as your ears. You may be surprised at what you'll learn.

MONTCLAIR
BAPTIST MEDICAL CENTER

Member of the Baptist Medical Centers System of Birmingham

A very informative ad (created by Lawler Ballard) on a very serious subject with visuals that graphically support the copy and assist the reader in taking away action-taking facts. A harder-working visual approach than the too common photos of kids taking, selling, or zonking out on drugs.

Magazine Ads that Work

Each year the Magazine Publishers Association asks an independent jury to pick the 25 best magazine ads of the year. One of these finalists is then chosen for their Kelly Award—the ad judged by industry professionals to represent the very best in magazine advertising.

The Kelly Award winner in 1990 was a color Nike ad (created by Wieden & Kennedy) with a very strong graphic presentation and spare, challenging copy.

SD Wild Animal Park

Across the world, on every continent, the wilderness is being taken away.

Not just from the animals.

From all of us, and our children.

But here, quietly tucked away in a valley north of San Diego, animals are being protected, babies are being born, life is flourishing.

Of the 42 endangered species living at the Wild Animal Park, 37 have reproduced here.

Come out on any given day, and at any given moment you could see something you've never seen before. And feel something you've never felt before.

Maybe you'll spot a pregnant Indian gaur, sitting alone, having separated herself from the herd. She knows that her time is due, and these things are best handled in private, between a mother and a baby.

Or you might see a just-born giraffe, all six feet of it, standing up and smelling the breeze for the first time.

And maybe, by the time that giraffe is 18 feet tall, and by the time your kids have kids, the world will be different.

And there won't be any more need for a place like this.

But until then, the flamingos will continue their slow, elaborate courtship dance.

And the wildebeests will continue to bark out to each other as the night falls.

And the sun will come up tomorrow.

And life will go on.

At the San Diego Wild Animal Park. The rarest of animals. In the rarest of places.

We hope you'll visit us and help us in our preservation efforts. If you want more information about the San Diego Wild Animal Park, please write to: San Diego Wild Animal Park, Dept. G-1, 15500 San Pasqual Valley Road, Escondido, CA 92027-9614.

The San Diego Wild Animal Park

We've recreated the wilderness in every detail. Except, that is, for the bulldozers, the land developers, and the poachers.

One of the 25 best. The dramatic color spread for the San Diego Wild Animal Park (created by Franklin & Associates) with appealing what-you-can-expect-when-you-visit-us copy.

Royal Viking Line

This handsome, fantasy provoking color spread for Royal Viking Line (created by Goodby, Berlin & Silverstein) was also a runner-up.

This hard-working color spread for Polaris, written as an adventure story (created by Carmichael Lynch, Inc) was another of the 25 best.

Absolut Vodka

And just to show that little or no copy can work in magazine space as it does on billboards, the 1990 Grand Effie winner (Effie stands for "Efficiency") from the American Marketing Association is this ad for Absolut Vodka (created by TBWA Advetising). Two of the fundamental reasons it works is (1) because of all that's gone before, and (2) the fact that there is no doubt about who the advertiser is.

The Bottom Line:

Each of the various print mediums has its own particular considerations that affect the character of the advertising therein. In all cases, however, check out the readability of the message. A superior creative idea will be rendered mediocre if it isn't inviting, easy to read, and perfectly clear in its message. A good way to start is to give any print ad, be it for a magazine or a newspaper, the billboard test. Does the ad register, even with fleeting attention, a positive idea while identifying your company or product with that idea?

So much for print. Let's have a look-hear at broadcast.

9

Creativity in Broadcast

Nobody goes there anymore, it's too crowded.
—Yogi Berra

Just to make the spot will cost $225,000. The viewer has cable and a satellite dish, a plethora of stations to tune in to and a bewilderment of advertising appeals to see each day. Your commercial had better be good.

In judging an idea, you have to go on faith. You've read the script, you've seen a storyboard, you may have even heard a scratch track of the music; but without investing a lot of preproduction money into simulating the final product, you can't be as sure as you can in print whether it's right. After all, in print you can see a tight comp that pretty much shows the way it will be. In broadcasting you've got a choice, roll the dice or think it through. Play roulette or play chess. It's your decision on whether what is being presented will deliver on what's being promised.

Approving a Television Commercial

When you're shown a storyboard for a TV commercial, you've got a couple of problems to overcome. First, there's the nature of the storyboard itself. A storyboard is a far cry from a finished commercial. You have to imagine how those funny little drawings in just those few boxes will translate into a finished mini moving picture. How it's shot, the director's vision, how the supers (the captions on screen) are handled, the casting, and a score of other major and minor details will greatly affect the ultimate potency of the spot. Your imagination, assisted by a full and clear explanation from those who will oversee its execution, must be in high gear.

119

The second problem you have to be aware of is that your interest in the commercial is quite naturally very high. For one thing, it's your product that's in the spotlight. For another, others are watching you for your reaction. You're on stage. Furthermore, you're totally focused on the commercial, and there are no other products' commercials or programming vying for your attention. Besides, the attention you will lavish on your proposed commercial can go on for some time, with rationales and salesmanship as part of the package. In short, this is not the real world. On the air no explanations will go along with its presentation: thirty seconds and it's all over. Never forget that the person you're trying to reach brings a wholly different frame of mind and attention span to viewing the spot on his or her set at home.

So before you commit to an opinion of the effectiveness of the commercial, wipe the slate clean and put yourself in the prospect viewer's couch in front of the TV. It's not easy. But it's very important that you work very hard at doing this, for these four good reasons:

1. The average consumer is exposed to some 50,000 commercials a year. Consider that in one hour of viewing time there could be up to 20 commercials on a single station. And don't forget, our overexposed consumer tuned in for a program, not a barrage of commercials. Between both, that's a lot of competition for attention.

2. You'll remember that I earlier noted that 70 percent of all commercials that come on screen, right in front of a viewer's nose, are ignored. That's right: 70 percent. And as was also mentioned, of those 30 percent of all commercials that get through, nearly 80 percent are misunderstood. Obviously too many viewers are nonattenders. Too many mentally switch off their minds without actually switching off the channel.

3. Then, of course, there are the zappers, those who switch stations when a commercial comes on. Advertisers have countered with both concentrated, high-frequency showings and with roadblocking (having the same commercial appear on a number of channels at the same time, forcing the viewer to see the commercial even if he or she clicks over to another channel).

4.   And mark this well: half of the people surveyed on how they
      feel in general about TV commercials said that most are
      usually in poor taste and very annoying.

Nobody promised you it was going to be easy.

Twelve Things to Watch Out For

1.   Watch out for any copy sequence that is complicated.

The very first thing to look for is that the message is simple and
clear. If you want to sell your house, put up a "For Sale" sign. You are
not presenting *Ben Hur*—you have only a handful of seconds, and it's
almost always better to concentrate on getting one key point across. A
complicated copy sequence will not register.

2.   Watch out for jolting incompatibilities.

Although your commercial may be simple and clear, consider
carefully whether it does indeed speak to your target audience.
Male-jock talk may work in selling a simonizing job, but I wouldn't
advise it for a feminine hygiene product. Nor would I advise a
hard rock sound track backing up a message to senior citizens, although it could well work in a spot aimed at teenagers. Know
who you're talking to if you want to strike a responsive chord. It's
just like real life. Julie isn't going to be sold if you say, "Judy,
I love you."

3.   Watch out for miscasting.

This is one of the make-or-break factors in a TV commercial. If
you've been wondering why they cast Kevin Costner rather than
Pee Wee Herman in Hollywood's latest romantic thriller, you're in
deep trouble. The actors, the celebrity personalities, the company
heads who appear in the commercial must be able to put the message
across in a style that is consistent with the concept. Look for acting
ability, believability, a twinkle in the eye, an engaging smile, a
bravura, a charming shyness—whatever will help make the message

work. Voice quality, while not being as absolutely vital as in radio, is extremely important and, when coupled with the right look and the right personality, can add immeasurably to the selling power of the spot.

4.   Watch out for inconsistent messages.

Consider your other advertising. If your campaign in television is consistent in both style and content with your radio and print advertising, you'll get extra clout.

5.   Watch out for words that you can't read on screen.

If you display supers in a TV commercial, make sure they're big enough to be read comfortably on a 13-inch screen as well as on a 36-inch ProjectaVision screen. And show the copy long enough so that those prospects who didn't earn honors in a speed-reading course can get it.

(Of course, legal copy that must be shown need only be as big, and on screen for as long, as the regulations insist. This is not very big and not very long. Although it's certainly important to lay out the caveats, this necessary copy can get in the way of your selling message; so don't make it any bigger than required, and don't keep it on any longer than required.)

6.   Watch out for any reference that the audience isn't privvy to.

Don't be lured into accepting inside jokes and hidden meanings. Never assume the viewer will get your point unless the key message is spelled out, so to speak, in capital letters.

7.   Watch out for talking down to your audience.

It is true that "America's Funniest Home Videos" is on prime time, while the meatiest talk shows and interviews are banished to Sunday morning's intellectual ghetto. And, you shouldn't permit your commercial to get complicated or too esoteric and sophisticated. Even so, be intelligent; flatter the audience, don't insult them. Although

H. L. Mencken said, "No one ever went broke underestimating the intelligence, or taste, of the American people," you are well advised to take this with a grain of salt.

8.   Watch out for cute kids, pets, celebrities, attractive models, funny jokes, music, and other elements that don't connect to the product.

They are message stealers. They draw attention to themselves. Even worse, they can actually put off the prospect. If one or several of these devices are in your intended commercial, make sure they link tightly, very tightly, to the product.

9.   Watch out for putting your competitor's name in your commercial.

It can lead to brand name confusion. Comparative, hard sell advertising can work, but consider it carefully. Usually you should resist the temptation. Make your brand name stand out above all else in the viewer's mind. Remember what Priscilla Mullins said: "Why don't you speak for yourself, John?" He did, and he, not the reluctant Miles Standish, got the order.

10.   Watch out for not having your brand or company name register.

The last things said are remembered more than the first things, so be sure that your key message and name are loud and clear at the end. Remember, though, that putting your name only at the end of a commercial can mean that your message is lost if the commercial gets zapped before then. Think about getting in your name at the start as well.

11.   Watch out for being bland, dull, or boring.

Entertainment is what television is all about, so be entertaining. No one is going to be very receptive to heavy-handedness and railing. A little show biz flair is necessary to interest prospects, particularly nonusers of the product or service being offered. But, as emphasized above, care must also be given to leave behind a strong, relevant, and believable message.

12. Watch out for throwing good money after bad.

Simply increasing advertising budgets does not necessarily have a positive impact on sales. What does work is improving the quality of the creative product. As was previously noted, the classic study of advertising effectiveness conducted by Booz Allen & Hamilton indicated that a superior creative idea can have up to 10 times the effectiveness of an ordinary idea.

What Works in TV Commercials

ASI Market Research, the world's largest communications research firm, concentrates its testing on TV commercials and programs. A commercial or program to be tested is broadcast via cable by ASI into respondents' homes over their own TV sets, so that the viewing happens normally. Telephone interviews follow, and the reactions from hundreds and hundreds of homes are tabulated by computer and analyzed.

Here are some elements that, according to ASI's testing of some nine hundred commercials over a two-year period between 1988 and 1990, get your commercial noticed:

humor
a happy or upbeat tone
a cute little kid, baby, or puppy
an ongoing character
a celebrity (the person's name must be mentioned in the commercial)

And here are some things that usually don't work as well:

a strong use of music
MTV-style approaches
mood commercials
a voice-over (as opposed to an on-screen presenter)
visual motion (moving camera, quick cuts, and so forth)
a message competing with music to be heard
copy or text appearing on-screen

These are overall guidelines. Any one of the positives could bomb badly. Likewise, any one of the negatives could work if handled correctly.

Understand that these findings apply to recall, that is, whether a commercial is noticed and remembered. Beyond this is the necessity of linking the name of the product advertised to the commercial remembered. ASI offers guidance in this area as well: "If there were a single rule for getting good levels of brand linkage, it would be to mention the name early and often, with audio mentions being considerably more important than visuals."

TV Commercials That Work

A winning commerical can take any of many forms. The elements that must come together to produce a winner will differ from spot to spot. In general, however, casting, direction, and production values almost without exception pay off. Over-production is a waste of budget. Skimping on called-for production is just as much, if not more, of a waste. Here are five quite different commercials all with a strong, if differing, mix of production values.

This Bounty commercial (created by Jordan, McGrath, Case & Taylor) is a dramatic change of pace from their "quicker picker upper" demo-in-the-diner spots of the past. If the earlier spots lacked charm their heavy repititions over the years gave a strong positioning to the product. This Mommy-and-Bounty-will-fix-it spot is emotional and heart-tugging and relates not only to mothers of young children but to all men and women who have ever had any relationship with a young child. Straight ahead photography of cute kids knocking over a glass or plate and then reacting with an about-to-burst-into-tears look backed with an appropriate, in-character song that goes, "I'm sorry, so sorry . . ."

Bounty

ANNOUNCER VOICE OVER: Bounty means never having to
SFX: (crash of cup of milk)
AVO: to say . . .
SONG: I'm sorry.

SFX: (bowl of spaghetti crashes to floor)
SONG: So sorry.
AVO: Even for the worst of spills.
SONG: I'm sorry.
SPOKEN VOICE: I'm sorry.
SFX: (egg falls and splatters on floor)
SONG: So sorry.
SPOKEN VOICE: So sorry. (sigh from Mom in background)
AVO: Bounty's quicker. And thicker than any other national 2-ply
paper towel. Bounty. The quicker, thicker, picker-upper.
SUPER: The Quicker *Thicker* Picker- Upper
AVO: Bounty means never having to say you're . . .
SUPER: Bounty Means Never Having To Say You're Sorry.
SONG: Sorry.

The Cola wars are waged with heavy artillery. The production values that went into the Pepsi Cola opera spot (created by BBDO) are superb. Michael J. Fox is in character which helps viewers follow the motivation of the action. Fox leaves his seat and date during an aria at the opera and goes out to the lobby for a Diet Pepsi. They're all sold out but he spots a machine outside on the street and gets his Diet Pepsi. Unfortunately, the door back in is locked but he gets back in through the stage door. Trapped until intermission he sits in a throne-like chair and sips his Diet Pepsi. Immediately the chair is thrust on stage as part of the action and Michael, surprised, relates to his date and the audience by raising his can of Diet Pepsi in a resigned salute. The product's importance to Fox and others of the Pepsi generation is amusingly exaggerated to an effective extreme.

Diet Pepsi

MUSIC: (opera arias throughout)
SUPER: Diet Pepsi. The Right One.

Honda as a piece of art is established vis a vis its engineering qualities in the Clio award-winning commercial included below (created by Rubin Postaer & Associates). A Honda is hung in a gallery. First a woman admires it then a man. The man walks up the wall, enters the car, and drives off. Overlaying the spot's arresting visual magic is a technical statement about the car that rubs off to the advertiser through the viewers admiring "how did they do that?"

Honda

MUSIC: (throughout) ANNOUNCER VOICE OVER AT END: You have to drive it to believe it. The new Accord.
SUPER: The new Accord. Honda.

Most airlines are, in their basic elements, essentially the same. It's the many little things that make the difference between one and another. This is a tricky area in which to be convincing. The Alaska Airlines Clio winning spot (created by Sedelmaier Film Productions) uses wonderfully offbeat characters, a Sedelmaier trademark, to make the point that they fuss the details for their customers' comfort. First, we see a big man and a small man in flight at night seated next to one another. The small man turns on his light and it focusses on the big man's arm. The big man stares at the small man who, cowed, trys to turn off his light. It won't go off. Next scene, day flight with a passenger struggling with his meal. It slides to him as the plane lurches. He pushes it back with one hand, adjusting his napkin with the other hand. Back and forth. A third scene shows a man by the sink in a cramped lavatory trying to get water out of the faucet. Suddenly it bursts forth and splashes all over the front of his pants. Just then the "Return To Seat" sign starts blinking urgently. Following these woeful scenes are some quick cuts of Alaska Airlines personnel tending to things: fixing a window shade, tidying the back of a seat, tightening a screw. Little details. Last shot is of the plane flying against a sunrise with the logo supered across the screen.

Alaska Airlines

ANNOUNCER VOICE OVER: Do the little things on your airline work as well as they should? (sequence of things going wrong)
Before you go on an Alaska Airlines airplane, we make sure everything is ship-shape . . . inside and out.
SUPER: Alaska Airlines (airplane flying in a sunrise sky)

Consistency is important in sports. It's hard to achieve in individual performance without consistency in the products that are part of the game. The Penn Tennis balls Clio winning commerical (created by Fallon McElligott) features a dramatic test to show off their you-can-count-on-it-consistent-quality. And as for the competition, their suggested point of difference is made with a dramatic, surprising, and humorous (if macabre) twist without naming names or actually doing a comparative test. After dropping a number of Penn Tennis balls 40 flights, all of which bounce to the same mark on the building, the announcer states that now they will try the same test with their competitor. At this point a man in a business suit is lifted by the two white-smocked laboratory technicians and dropped over the side of the building.

Penn

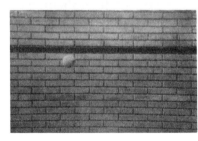 

ANNOUNCER VOICE OVER: How do Penn Tennis balls compare with our nearest competitor?
We'll drop three Penn Tennis balls from the top of a forty story building.

You can see that even for forty stories, each ball bounces to the same height every time.
Now we try the same test with our competitor. (Technicians pick up second tester man and throw him over edge of building.)
Penn Tennis balls. You've seen one. You've seen them all.
SUPER: Penn. You've seen one. You've seen them all.

Approving a Radio Commercial

It's here, there, and everywhere. It's with you when you're sitting, when you're standing, when you're lying down, when you're on the run, and even when your eyes are closed. Unlike TV viewers, who sit down in front of their sets and essentially watch only at home, or magazine and newspaper readers, who also give reasonably close attention to what they're looking at, radio listeners tend to be doing something else while they listen: driving their cars, jogging, working in the office, or cooking a meal at home.

This is very important. Odd as it may seem at first blush, radio has a lot in common with billboards, because both mediums are attended to when people are doing something else.

A Four Point Alert

In general what was said about TV can be applied to evaluating radio commercials. But be particularly insistent on the following points:

1. Keep it simple. Sure, you've got 60 seconds, but if you try to unload too much freight, nothing is going to register. Unlike billboards, TV, or magazines and newspapers, the reinforcement and clarification of visuals are not part of the process. So be clear, concise, and to the point. Don't try to do too much.

2. Drum home your key message and product name. It's virtually impossible to overdo this. Repeat the principal point at least once. If you have an 800 number, work it in three times in close proximity at or near the end. Obviously, a mnemonic 800 number greatly aids retention. 800-BUY-FAST may well be

remembered even if said only once. 800-289-3278 may not register with even three repeats.

3.   Make a memorable exit. Even more so than in TV, in radio the key point has a much better chance of registering if it comes at the end. Again, remember that in radio you have no visuals. You can't show a logo. The last thing heard has the potential to be remembered best. Be certain that you have a strong connection to both your selling premise and your company or product name at the end.

See to it that these first three points—simplicity, repetition, and a memorable brand/company ending—are covered in your spot. They're the fundamental underpinnings of a commercial that will deliver value for the money you put into it. However, be very much aware that the variations and permutations on how you achieve your goal are infinite. This is where creativity, structured on that rearrangement of old ideas, comes in.

4.   A final, critically important point: the secret of judging a radio script is to hear it. Print copy is written for the eye, but radio copy is written for the ear. Never make a judgment on a script after having read it silently to yourself. Have it read to you. At least read it aloud to yourself. Listen to how it plays. Imagine the voices, the music, the sound effects. Listen with your third ear to what the finished spot might be like.

Four Basic Approaches (and Four Things to Watch Out For)

There are some distinctive, classic directions to take in crafting a radio commercial that will win attention:

Slice of Life

You've seen them on television, you've heard them on radio. Short playettes that mimic real-life situations.

What to watch out for: Beware of copy that sounds like it was taped by "Candid Recorder." In general, you don't want dialogue that comes straight out of actual life. It's certainly true that nobody talks the way they do in slice-of-life commercials. But that's okay. We've only got 60 seconds, and we've got to telescope reality into those few moments. Just be aware that the slice-of-life approach generally works better on TV. On radio the dialogue, without supporting visuals, can sound ridiculous and be a real turnoff. Using wit and humor (see below) is one way around this problem (although serious, well-acted, and creatively conceived and written spots can also be very effective). But whatever the character of the slice-of-life spot, the quality of the dialogue and the casting are critical.

Humor

Some of the most memorable radio commercials over the years have been those that provoked a giggle or a guffaw. A humorous commercial can get and hold a listener's attention. It can make a person feel good.

What to watch out for: Make sure the humor hooks to the product. Often humorous commercials don't connect to the product or company, and no matter how much of a rib-tickler, the spot has to be labeled a flop. The key message and product name cannot play second banana to the fun. Remember that you're selling a product, not producing a sitcom, a vaudeville show, or a night at Catch a Rising Star.

The jingle

There have been some highly memorable musical signatures that, have in and of themselves brought the product to mind and have even evoked some powerful emotions concerning it. Music can most definitely strike the right chord with your target market.

What to watch out for: One of the legendary leaders of one of America's better-known advertising agencies once said, "If you have nothing to say, sing it." A message that is sung can be buried in the lyrics, the brass, or the timpani. There's a better-than-ever chance that a convincing voice, speaking with clarity and emphasis, can communicate the same information with more authority. But there are a few things to keep in mind when using music. If the music is behind the spoken voice, it must not intrude, and it must be in a mood that is compatible with the message. If featured prominently, it must have a distinctive quality about it—if even no more than a "doot doot," as in the music composed many years back for Beneficial Finance's spots, or the "thump thump" rhythm in Chevrolet's "Heartbeat of America" commercials.

Music does not have to be originally composed for the spot, although this is frequently done. Here are two classic examples of music that was borrowed and made the advertiser's own:

In the mid-1950s Marlboro bought the rights to the theme from the western classic *The Magnificent Seven* and, with the help of some exciting cinematography, changed a woman's cigarette into a macho, male brand. It hasn't been on radio or TV for more than a decade, but the melody is embedded in smokers' (and nonsmokers') heads, and many are reminded of it whenever they see a photo of a rugged cowboy.

Back in radio's golden years, Silvercup Bread sponsored "The Lone Ranger," whose theme song was the overture to Rossini's opera *William Tell*. To this day it's hard for anyone over 40 not to think of, "Hi-yo Silver, away!" when hearing it. Note that the horse's name is Silver, a crafty, creative mnemonic for the product name.

A caution: once composed or selected, the quality of the music and the production values put into creating the final, performed piece are extremely important. Don't stint here.

Sale

Everyone likes a bargain. Retail advertisers especially use radio very effectively in announcing price cuts.

What to watch out for: Don't hem, haw, hedge, fudge, or dance around what you have to say. Solid, specific data on the magnitude of the sale and the sale prices are useful, compelling information. So tell your prospects. They'll be all ears if you do it right. Make sure you're generating excitement. Treat the sale as important news, and inject a clear note of urgency. But don't bubble and screech beyond all believability, and don't get so caught up in creating excitement and enthusiasm that you forget to lay out the values of the product itself.

The Voice of Persuasion

There are other elements that can go into a radio commercial. But whatever the style and content, nothing is more critical to the success of a radio commercial than casting—the voice or voices you use for the spot. The right talent (I blush to say) can even carry a mediocre concept and script. The wrong talent can diminish or even totally negate a well-conceived approach. The important thing to keep in mind in radio is that you are relying on voice alone—principally in an announcement by a spokesperson or dialogue, but also in music—without any visual character or personality, to deliver your message. Instrumental music and sound effects can play an important role in the process, but it's the voice that carries the words you want to communicate.

When approving the casting, look for warmth and friendliness: a voice that suggests a pleasant, reliable person. Certain character parts, of course, may call for a different projection. And be sure, no matter how mellifluous or on-target the voice is, that the person can act. You want someone who can get a point across convincingly.

In using humor, of course, the voice may have some different qualities. If our chosen talent can make someone laugh, that someone is apt to feel good about the product being advertised. The basic selling premise of making friends, not enemies, is always operative, whatever the nature of the spot.

Radio Scripts that Work

Here are five award-winning radio scripts that worked hard to sell each of the company's products. It is very difficult to read a script and judge the final product. A script should be read aloud with attention to how it tracks, the clarity of the key message, and its inherent potential to be carried by the production elements (actors, music, sound effects).

For example, the Motel 6 commerical (created by The Richards Group) certainly reads well enough in type but in its finished on-air form it works to perfection because of the casting. It is hard to imagine the commercial being as warm and successful as it is with a different voice, a different delivery, and different music. The Motel 6 series can boast of Clio awards with this specific spot picking up the Gold from two other award shows.

MOTEL 6 SCRIPT

Hi, Tom Bodett for Motel 6 and I'm here to wax a little philosophic. You know, at Motel 6 we have a philosophy: People sleep, therefore, we are. And the way we figure it, since you don't appreciate artwork when you're sleepin', why hang it in the rooms. I guess if you wanted to be technical though, our walls can be considered art. Abstract art. You know, nothing to get in the way of individual interpretation. Sort of like an empty canvas to be painted on with the mind. Holy smokes, that's deep. I'd just better do the commercial. At Motel 6, you get just what you need. A clean, comfortable room and a good night's sleep for around 22 bucks in most places. A little more in some, and a lot less in others, but always the lowest prices of any national chain and always a heck of a deal. It's a simple philosophy, but it makes good sense. Sort of like a rolling stone not gatherin' any moss. Or that bird in the hand stuff. Ah, I think you get the drift. I'm Tom Bodett, art critic, for Motel 6 and we'll leave the walls bare for you.

Another commercial carried by just one single voice is the Laughing Cow spot (created by Joy Radio). The actor's accent and the rhythm of her delivery perfectly complements the uninhibited Valley Girl zaniness of the script to make the listener smile (if not burst out laughing) and remember the product. Both the client and Joy Radio are laughing all the way to the trophy case with a load of awards including Clios, Andys, and an Effie.

LAUGHING COW SCRIPT

VALLEY GIRL:
So like I was driving down the Freeway, ok. And this totally gorgoso highway patrolman stops me. So I said like wow there's wheels on your motorcycle and wheels on my car. I mean that's really Kharmoso. He said you were speeding. I said I have to get my little round Laughing Cow in the red net bag into the fridge ok. He said where's the cow. I said in the trunk, ok. He said you're not authorized to carry livestock. I said officer that is like really heavy. The Laughing Cow isn't like a real cow ok it's like cheese, ok. Mild Mini Bonbel, Nippy Mini Babybel, and new Mini Gouda. You know like really awesome and naturelle. Five delicious round cheeses in little net bags. Each one wrapped like in wax with a cute little zip thing. He said open the trunk. I said ok. He said you need a key. I mean like this guy was totally brilliant ok. I said you want a little Laughing Cow? So he said ok. So I said ok. So we said ok, ok. So then he asked me for my license. And I said when can I see you again. He was so totally freaked like he dropped the cheese and bit the ticket. So now it's two weeks and he never called.

The Delta script (created by Bert & Barz) lives or dies on how the spot works because the intentionally exaggerated characters underline the fun and appeal of Delta's kids-oriented program. And, of course, it works because the client put their tongue securely in cheek, didn't get literal, and went with the concept.

DELTA AIR LINES SCRIPT

SFX: AIRLINER IN-FLIGHT
WOMAN: Welcome aboard Delta.
KID: Hi, I'm Michael and this is my little brother Howard.
MAN: (Deep Voice) Call me, "Howie"
WOMAN: Little brother?

MAN: Uh, we'd like to be Delta Fantastic Flyers, please.
WOMAN: But that's just for kids 2-12.
KID: I'm 7.
MAN: And I'm uh, 8.
WOMAN: When were you born?
MAN: Nineteen for . . . uh, 80.
WOMAN: Well, you're pretty tall for 8.
MAN: It's these elevator sneakers.
WOMAN:*And* you need a shave.
MAN: Oh, too many vitamins in my lollipop.
WOMAN: Lollipop?
KID: (To Woman) Howie's trying to give up cigars.
WOMAN: You just want to get a free Mickey Mouse visor . . .
MAN: And the Fantastic Flyer magazine . . .
KID:. . . With all the neato stories, puzzles and games.
MAN: Me and my son Michael think it's rad.
WOMAN: Son?
MAN: I mean brother.
KID: We're twins.
MAN: Fraternal.
WOMAN: I think you're older than 8.
MAN: How about 9?
WOMAN: You have a bald spot.
MAN: Well, I've had that since I was 20. Oops.
ANNCR: When kids 2-12 fly Delta they can join Delta's Fantastic
Flyer Program. After enrollment they receive a free membership
certificate, poster, button and a subscription to Fantastic Flyer
magazine, with chances to win free trips. No purchase required.
MAN: Son, it's my turn to wear the Mickey Mouse visor.
KID: Unh-unh.
MAN: I'll let you play with my brief case.
KID: Forget it, Howie.
ANNCR: Delta. The official airline for kids.

AT&T, as you are probably well aware by now, sells an idealized
America. Family, friends, romantic love. In this spot (created by Chuck
Blore & Don Richman) a young man self-consciously calls a young

woman for a date. The tenderness and humor of the situation come solidly through because the script is believable and catches the moment. Again, the casting carries it. The actors play it with just the right real life touch which helps simulate the effect of the listener "eavesdropping" on what seems to be a conversation actually taking place. The spot was a double Clio award winner.

AT&T SCRIPT

CATHIANNE: Hello.

DANNY: Uh, hi. You probably still remember me, Edward introduced us at the seminar . . .

CATHIANNE: Oh, the guy with the nice beard.

DANNY: I don't know whether it's nice . . .

CATHIANNE: It's a gorgeous beard.

DANNY: Well, thank you, uh, listen, I'm gonna, uh, be in the city next Tuesday and I was, y'know wondering if we could sorta, y'know, get together for lunch?

CATHIANNE: How 'bout dinner?

DANNY: Dinner? Dinner! Dinner's a better idea. You could pick your favorite restaurant and . . .

CATHIANNE: How 'bout my palce? I'm my favorite cook.

DANNY: Uh, your place. Right, Sure.That's great to me.

CATHIANNE: Me too. It'll be fun.

DANNY: Yeah . . . listen, I'll bring the wine.

CATHIANNE: Perfect. I'll drink it.

BOTH: (Laugh)

DANNY: Well, O.K., then, I guess it's a date. I'll see you Tuesday.

CATHIANNE: Tuesday. Great.

DANNY: Actually, I just, uh, I called to see how you were and y'know, Tuesday sounds fine!

SOUND:*Phone Hangs Up*

DANNY: (Yelling) Tuesday . . . Ahhhh . . . she's gonna see me Tuesday (Fade)

SUNG: REACH OUT, REACH OUT AND TOUCH SOMEONE (Fade)

There's enough of the way little girls really are in this script to give this humorous commercial (created by Dick Orkin's Radio Ranch) the charm that makes it special. This is also a very hard-working, award-winning spot (The International Broadcast Awards Grand Sweepstakes Winner) with the advertiser's name mentioned nine times and seven different kinds of candy identified to tempt the listener. If that isn't enough, the fact that Brachs can be bought at Carr's is repeated four times. A lot of freight but the way it is handled it all registers.

BRACHS SCRIPT

MISSY: Hi, Mr. Fletcher.
MR. F: Oh, Hi Missy.
MISSY: I'm Missy, The little girl who lives next door.
MR. F: I know who you are, Missy.
MISSY: What's in the bag?
MR. F: Just some stuff from Carrs.
MISSY: What kind of stuff?
MR. F: Oh, well there's like Brachs candy . . .
MISSY: Candy?
MR. F: Yeah, Brachs candy. It's new at Carrs . . .
MISSY: My mommy says I should always share my candy.
MR. F: Well, okay pick a piece of Brach's candy from my bag here . . .
MISSY: What's this?
MR. F: Chocolate Creme.
MISSY: What's this?
MR. F: Gudinger Ball.
MISSY: What's this?
MR. F: A Milk Maid Caramel.
MISSY: What's this?
MR. F: Tell you what, how bout a Brachs lolly drop?
MISSY: Okay.
MR. F: Well, bye . . .
MISSY: Can I have one to share with my sister?

MR. F: Okay.
MISSY: What's this?
MR. F: A Butterscotch Disk.
MISSY: What's this?
MR. F: A Mint Creme.
MISSY: What's . . .
MR. F: How bout a nice Brachs Rainbow Bear for your sister.
MISSY: Uhhhhh . . .
MR. F: Missy, I really have to go in the house now.
MOM: Is Missy bothering you, Mr. Fletcher?
MR. F: Oh, no I was just giving her a piece of the Brachs candy I got at Carrs.
MOM: Brachs candy.
MR. F: Yeah, Carrs has a new pick and mix display with 16 different flavors.
MOM: Ohhh . . .
MR. F: Would you like a piece?
MOM: Oh, sure . . . what's this?
MR. F: Oh, no . . .
MOM: What's this?
ANNCR: Brachs candies. New at Carrs. In a variety of sizes and flavors to fit you taste. Nobody treats America like Brachs.

The Bottom Line

Sure, provide information. But also always think show business when you advertise on TV or radio. You're at bat for a matter of seconds— usually 30 on television and 60 on radio. Sometimes you buy even less. So get to the point and keep it simple. Make sure it's a hit.

What is said is vital. But in both TV and radio, the who that's saying it and how it is being said can make or break the idea. Great ideas have been killed by the wrong casting, but ordinary ideas can get a big lift from brilliant casting. Pay attention to production values—the images in TV and the characterizations, voice, and music on both TV and radio. And register your company name.

10

Choosing A Creative Agency

You cannot fly like an eagle with the wings of a wren.
—William Henry Hudson

Before you go through the process of choosing an agency to work with you, be fully aware that whomever you decide to shake hands with will only be as good as you allow. A client must be open, cooperative, accessible, and supportive. You, or your interfacing staff, must not work at arm's length with the agency (or your free-lancers) just so you can disassociate yourself from the agency if something goes wrong. If you do, something surely will go wrong.

The trickiest part of the whole process is being as perceptive and objective as you can in judging the agency's ability to put creative thinking to work for you. The easier part, though it too can be a minefield, is determining which group has the right chemistry for you. Both parts of the equation are very, very important. You absolutely must not sacrifice creative credentials for chemistry. And you absolutely must not work with those who appear to be enormously creative if you don't like them a lot. Between the two essentials, creativity and chemistry, you are clearly left somewhere between playing God and being on The Dating Game in this whole process of choosing with whom you will work.

The Courtship

It's as if you're a bachelor millionaire. It's a flirtation, and the chase is on. Everyone is smiling, attentive, full of enthusiasm for you and your

product. "We'll make beautiful music together." Of course it's flattering. You're being promised anything and everything, and you have all
those proposals to mull over. No other professional help with which
you choose to work is held up to the same scrutiny: not your doctor,
your lawyer, your accountant, or your baby-sitter. Just don't get
seduced by it all. This is business, very serious business. The
hard-nosed question you have to examine is, Which marriage partner
will live up to the courtship?

Don't Ignore the Girl Next Door

If you live in Georgia, you're not going to seek out and buy peaches
from California when shopping at the produce store. Consider first
whether the best agency isn't the one right in front of you, as obvious
as a pit in an avocado. Don't complicate the situation. Let's say that
you know one of the owners and have always admired his keenness,
style, and enthusiasm. You've heard good things about the work his
agency is turning out. What you've seen of it strikes you as being
especially smart and creative. In that case, hire them. Save yourself a
lot of time and a lot of agonizing effort.

Maybe there are two or three local agencies that could be right.
Look at them all. Play the field, and put the guidelines that follow to
work for you and make your choice.

As a matter of fact, the principle of saving your time and effort goes
for your present agency as well. When you think that you may need a
change, sit down first with the principals and have a heart-to-heart. If
they are bright and responsive, they'll make some internal shifts
(perhaps a different account supervisor or a fresh creative team) that
will give you in effect a new agency. Let them know exactly how you
feel and where you see the problem. And keep an open mind on what
your shortcomings in the relationship might have been. But remember, if you don't think much of the leadership and direction coming
from the top, forget the whole thing, and start looking for another
agency.

The Selection Process

There are a number of traditional ways to go about a search, such as
distributing questionnaires to the candidates, and having the screen-

ing committee fill out evaluation scales. They have their place, but at best they are a prelude to where your attention should be focused if you're expecting action-provoking creativity. When faced with a roster of candidates, some of these standard screening procedures may help you cut down the list to a manageable two or three, which is where you want to get as quickly as possible. But in the overall process thorough examination of ability is more important than the skin-deep impressions gained from generalized formulas. When faced with a roster of candidates, some of these standard screening procedures may help you cut down the list to a manageable two or three, which is where you want to get as quickly as possible if you're expecting action-provoking creativity.

Make clear which person, whether you or someone else, will be responsible for choosing or for directing the choosing of the new agency. Give that person both the authority to come to a recommendation and a firm timetable for doing it. Others in your company will surely be involved, but for an orderly and businesslike use of everyone's time, the process is best put in the hands of one responsible, qualified person. Depending on the complexity of the problem and the people who are available, three to six weeks are generally sufficient. Longer time frames tie up your executives and managers and dissipate their attention. It is very difficult to efficiently and objectively make a competitive evaluation when the process is spread over too many weeks.

The selection person must be absolutely clear about what he or she is looking for in an agency. It is essential to determine at the outset those desirable characteristics you want in your agency. All this is so obvious and fundamental that it's often taken for granted and overlooked. At the same time, be sure you don't burden yourself with arbitrary and rigid requirements. You must be reasonable and flexible if the goal is sizzling creativity.

Six Considerations

1. Conflicts

It is usually a good policy not to place your business at an agency that is working for a competitor and intends to continue doing so. Of course, an agency with a conflicting account may refuse to talk with you, citing the conflict. Or they may wish to compete for the business on the understanding that they'll leave the competitor if they start working for you because your budget is larger. You'll have to judge whether the first response indicates a sense of contractual integrity or a shortfall of aggressiveness, or whether the latter response indicates an unbecoming lack of loyalty to their client or an understandable wish to move up in challenge and reward. If you do choose to include an agency with a competing account in your evaluation (of course, the definition of competing accounts is not always as clear as Coke and Pepsi), do so only if you have greatly admired what they have done for your competitor. Then you must evaluate the pros of their knowing your industry and the cons of their possibly having shot their best idea on the campaign you so admire.

2. Resources

Determine whether each agency you look at has the resources to provide you with expertise and backup. Backup is very important. Just because one person on the agency's staff has had some experience in an area particularly close to your heart doesn't mean the agency can consistently provide sophisticated, effective assistance in that area. One-man bands are rather limited in their repertoires.

3. Related experience

An agency doesn't have to have worked extensively in your industry area, although that may be helpful. Having experience in a related area can be just as good. Good marketing thinking is transferable. The important thing to look for is intelligence and range in solving problems. You don't want an agency with one act. An agency specializing in real estate, travel, fashion, pharmaceuticals, or finance may have the advantage of knowing the industry's rules at the start-up, but it will have creative disadvantages as well. If an agency consistently shows initiative and imagination in solving the needs of its clients, put them on your short list. After all, you know the business cold. You want an agency that will work with you as a partner; has the talent and smarts to translate your wisdom, learn from it, and add to it; and knows how to push the right psychological buttons that will help you sell to your market.

4. Convenience

Long-distance relationships can work. The fax, the modem, and the telephone can literally put client and agency in the same room in minutes. But all other things being equal, the ability to have regular face-to-face working sessions (sometimes on short notice) has its advantages. Look close to home first, as noted above. The grass may look greener in the other pasture, but it usually isn't.

There may be good reasons for an out-of-town agency: in certain situations an agency in New York, with direct access to the largest talent pool and the publishing and broadcast industries, could be a real advantage. Likewise a Houston agency may have a real leg up in working with the oil industry. The same would be true for a Seattle agency working with the aviation industry or a Los Angeles agency serving the movie industry. In such situations you'll have to evaluate whether you want to work with an agency's headquarters or with their branch office. A nearby branch office is convenient and is essentially a separate, competitive, local agency.

5. Run through the numbers

How many people are handling how much business? Remember to consider account activity, not just billing. A large account may generate two or three commercials a year. A small account may demand an ad a week. Look for steady but not necessarily spectacular growth. If an agency has been hot, winning account after account, they could be overextended. It takes time to add superior people, to get them working in harmony with the agency culture, and for management to expand internal systems. And, of course, you are well advised to check out the financial stability of any agency you are seriously interested in.

It is important, if you would represent less than 5 percent of the agency's billing, to consider whether you might be too small to matter. You want top-executive involvement when you need it. If contrarily you represent 50 percent or more of their billing, remember that the agency is not being stimulated by a variety of challenges. The cross-fertilization of ideas gained from working with a variety of industries can be to your advantage. Be aware of the agency's vulnerability in this regard if you might want to make a change in the future. Such vulnerability, you may feel as a properly sensitive, responsible business executive, could inhibit you from making a beneficial switch.

6. Track record

If an agency's client list includes a high percentage of long-term clients, that's good. Even better is evidence of the significant growth of a client during that client's association with the agency. Such growth may or may not have been largely of the agency's doing, but it certainly suggests an effective working partnership. It's important to call the references and have a few minutes' chat. They'll probably say good things, so probe a little. Ask about the agency's responsiveness and innovativeness. Especially find out if these clients think that the agency is creatively adventuresome: do they stick their necks out to make things happen? Just remember not to take the responses you get as infallible or be surprised by inconsistencies. If you ask each of the more than 500 religious sects in the world to describe the nature of God, you'll get 500 different answers.

You can efficiently screen agency candidates by sensibly using the above techniques. Narrow down your list with a formal questionnaire if that suits your sense of meticulousness. But use it as a first-cut pruning tool. Follow the above six points in profiling the candidates. Keep it simple; these basics need not get complicated. Once you have considered an agency in view of the six points, the criteria you should focus most of your time and attention on are (1) the agency's creative talent and (2) the agency's people compatability with you and your company. The fundamental six points will help you get a well-run, professional organization. These latter two considerations will help you get advertising that works.

Judging What's Creative

I could write out a checklist of things to look for that indicate creativity. I could even assign weighted points to each and index the total to a Scale of Relative Creativity. I could, but it wouldn't be accurate, helpful, or reflective of the real world. The annual advertising awards, chosen by industry professionals, do not necessarily represent the most compelling, effective advertising. What they do represent are those ads, chosen from the relatively small number of advertisements that are submitted to these competitions, that the judges find appealing. Sometimes the winners represent hardworking ads that sell, but sometimes they don't. Hard facts and proof of what works and what doesn't are as difficult to come by as gold nuggets in the pan of a treasure hunter sifting pebbles from a stream. What I can do to help is suggest how you can be as impartial as possible in making judgments on creative work.

Remember, trust your own creative sense. You can and must make some subjective appraisals of the work you'll be seeing. The annoying, puzzling, and very delicate part of finding the agency that will give you the creativity that will help make things happen is the issue of what is creative. Keep in mind that you shouldn't get blown away by the outrageous. Being outrageous, being different for the sake of being different is not, as noted previously, the absolute, never-failing basis of creative advertising. Being creative is finding the right balance of appeal and presence that will help produce sales. Creative advertising certainly gets one's attention and has a burr of singularity about it. But the end purpose is to help sell. The most important thing to look for is a message that is understandable, persuasive, and clearly identifiable as yours.

There is a mystique and promise about creative advertising that fascinates advertisers (as it should). However, to emphasize it again, creative advertising is advertising that stirs things up and provokes action. Such persuasions are virtually always built on clear, purposeful straight-on propositions. The objective of your advertising isn't to collect raves about the advertising itself (although that's flattering and impresses management), but to create desires for your product or service.

Media, research, and account management are all very, very

important pieces in the mosaic. But nothing is more important than creativity.

Pruning the List

Use the six fundamental points described above to narrow down your choices to just two or three agencies. The longer the list, the more difficult to get the feel of the finalists. Remember, don't resist if you find early on what clearly appears to be the right agency for you. Go for it. David O. Selznick didn't audition an army of actors for the role of Rhett Butler. He knew who was right from the outset.

The best way to evaluate creativity is to ask the agency for a credentials presentation. Ask that they show a sampler of their work for all present and recent clients. If it is a large agency with many accounts, limit the number to 10 or 12 clients. Include the names of any specific accounts you particularly wish to see. In your request for this credentials presentation, make it clear that you expect them to speak to what they perceive to be your needs and to explain in a few minutes, their thinking in crafting the creative approach for each advertisement.

After the presentation, speak to at least six clients. Ask how the agency's creative suggestion was developed. Did the client buy it right away? Was the agency firm but not boorish in pushing for the advertising they presented? Did they believe in it? And (the key question) did it work? If it didn't work, it wasn't sales-smart, make-it-happen creative.

Reviewing the work is extremely important. It deserves a generous portion of your time and analysis. In the long run this method of evaluation, concentrating on the product, will get you a better agency in a shorter time. So don't complicate things. You can go through the review of fundamental facts and figures with minimum effort and fanfare. Save your time and resources to look closely at the creative product of, preferably, just two or three agencies. Be sure to pinpoint the work you like and ascertain that the people who created the work are still at the agency and will work on your account.

The Trouble with Speculative Presentations

Speculative presentations (where the agencies show off print or broadcast advertising created for your product) should be outlawed by an act of Congress. They are blackmail, an imposition, an illusion. Ask three accounting firms to prepare your taxes, and tell them you will only pay the one who gets you the biggest refund. Lots of luck. And don't say you're willing to pay the agency for the speculative presentation. The amount is always a fraction, a small fraction, of what it costs an agency to mount a competitive presentation. We on the agency side should be working for our clients, putting our effort into helping them with ever-better and ever-stronger ideas.

From the client's perspective, what is being measured is an agency's one-shot effort. It's a test of the agency's show biz abilities: the most persuasive presentation, not necessarily the best idea, wins. From the agency's point of view, it's like picking which cup the pea is under. They pick up one of the three cups, and there it is! So they get the assignment. They may never get it right again. There is no guaranteed relationship between making a good presentation and making good advertising.

To be fair, there is a positive side to the speculative creative presentation. You can see firsthand how each prospective agency reacts to the challenge, to a specific problem. You can judge their resourcefulness and the range and inventiveness of their creative ideas. But you can test this more effectively, with less chance of mishap, by thoroughly reviewing and discussing a broad range of their creative work, as suggested.

One basic problem, besides the fact that for the agency a speculative presentation is like a shell game, is that an agency faced with preparing a speculative presentation rarely has enough time to gain proper insights and knowledge to fully appreciate the problem. If it's a well-run agency, there isn't a lot of deadwood around. To mount a speculative presentation, they must take time away from their present clients, if and when they can. This gives an agency in a slow period an unfair advantage over an agency that happens to be in the midst of a major creative effort for one or more clients.

Also, an agency can subcontract the task to free-lancers, who often work for a good number of agencies on a hired gun basis. The people

who work on the speculative presentation will not necessarily be the
regular, continuing individuals on your account. Just as with already-
produced agency work that you admire, ask who exactly developed
the speculative ideas.

The Importance of Chemistry

The other important criterion to consider after creativity, as stated
earlier, is the character of the people with whom you are thinking of
working. How comfortable are you with them? Do you genuinely like
and respect them? Chemistry, you must keep in mind, is fundamental
in getting provocative creativity, time after time, on time and on
budget. You may have noticed that Fred and Ginger didn't step on
each other's toes. The people you want are those who will listen to
you. Likewise, you will feel confident in listening to them. They will
be responsive and will respect you. They will include you in their
thinking at every step and will be confident that they can go to the
edge, take some risks, and get your support.

Chemistry is certainly something you can feel; trust those feelings.
But check up on yourself. After all, you didn't get married after the
first date. Go to the agency at least twice. The first time is for the
credentials presentation. The second time, go on short notice, since
you don't want the agency to be artificially staged for your visit. You
want to see the agency as close to the way it really is as possible. When
you make the appointment, tell your prospective working partners
that you want to have some short one-on-one visits with several of the
people who would be working on the account should you assign it to
that agency. Talk to the day-to-day art director and the day-to-day
copywriter. Talk to their immediate supervisors. Ask that your proposed account supervisor orchestrate the visit and act as host. You
don't have to spend a lot of time. Play it by ear, but certainly spend at
least 10 minutes with each person. See what they're working on; get a
feel for what makes them tick; take note of how they relate to their
colleagues and how they answer the phone. And spend some time
with the agency principals. Tell them about your visits and reactions.
See how they respond. Find out how they feel about their own people.
You want to feel very comfortable with the people who run the agency
as well.

A Word on Leadership

In every organization, business, political, or religious, it all starts at the top. As with your company, an agency's character is a reflection of the style and philosophy of its leaders. Agencies whose top management are practicing creative types are more likely to deliver sizzling, on-target, creative advertising than agencies whose top management came up through marketing, account management, research, or finance. Agencies that are publicly owned or have gone through megamergers or are owned by a larger agency are much more likely to be focused on profit margins (and bonuses), while creatively led, independent, entrepreneurial agencies tend to focus on cost-efficient, highly effective ads.

This is not to suggest that smaller agencies are per se financially immature. And keep an open mind about large agencies, too. Some creative units in large agencies and some branch office agencies are blessed with highly creative people who are encouraged to foster their entrepreneurial spirit.

Look for Visual Impact

Another thing to look for is an agency with an art director who is a genuine creative star. A copywriter creative star who has strong graphic sensitivity is also very desirable. Agencies that build their advertising on a strong visual base are apt to make fresher, more memorable, more attention-getting advertising than those that don't.

Print and television advertising make their first impact visually. And remember, an advertisement's first duty is to get itself read (or seen and heard). An ad's presence is all-important. Art directors, by their very nature and training, are focused on presence and presentation. The best of them think instinctively of how to appeal to the eye. They are able to turn a concept into a graphic format that captures and directs attention to the selling premise of the print or broadcast advertisement. The gifted copywriter focuses on putting the concept into words, but it's the art director who controls visual emphasis and style.

The art director almost always spends considerably more time on a given piece than a copywriter. Typically copy can be developed in a matter of hours. The layout, with all its elements of typography, photography, and illustration, can take days to weeks to complete. Art directors are therefore more in control of the development and final character of the ad or TV commercial.

Even radio commercials can be produced to be seen in the mind's eye. This is desirable when radio commercials run in conjunction with TV spots. When properly constructed, the radio spot will suggest the images that the listener has seen in the television advertisements.

The best manager of a creative department, however, is not necessarily an art-trained person. Historically more head creative directors have come up through copy. However, an art person or a copy person can be a successful creative leader. It all depends on the individual's personality and leadership qualities, how concept-driven he or she is and the corporate culture of the agency.

As noted above, in the best of all creative worlds art directors and copywriters work together from the initial conception stages right through to the end. Almost invariably this is the way to produce the strongest, most creative advertising. In reviewing an agency, check to see to what extent a collaborative working style is built into the agency structure. Realize that the best copywriters are those who are very visually oriented, and the best art directors are those who are very verbally oriented. A crackerjack creative team is possessed by and obsessed with this reciprocal reinforcing of talent.

Copywriters who have not been trained in graphic art often have a difficult time in actually crafting the visual aspects of a print ad. Art directors, like most educated people, are able to write reasonably well, and, if possessed of any initiative and conviction, have no hesitation in suggesting changes in a copywriter's work or even inventing whole new approaches. The copywriter has to be content to keep suggesting, describing, and pushing for the visual approaches in his or her mind's eye. To insure that each person's particular talent is used productively, a strongly cooperative, collaborative working relationship between art and copy people is essential.

The Bottom Line

Look for an agency whose leadership comes from the creative end of the business. Be skittish about agencies led exclusively by a professional account or administrative specialist. Certainly be suspicious of a leader who came up through financial management. Unless, of course, a strong creative personality helps that leader shape the agency's philosophy. A financially trained person is essential to a well-run agency, but as the guiding light setting the tone, such a person is likely to emphasize the business nitty-gritty at the expense of creativity. Obviously, both business and art are important. Neither can be shortchanged if you are looking for sizzling creativity.

Focus your energies and attention on the work produced by the agency you're considering. Make sure the work was created by people who are still there. Look at it carefully. Listen to it. See if it resonates in your gut. Then talk to at least three of the agency's clients closest to your size and situation. Find out firsthand whether advertising the agency has produced for them works. Have confidence in your own creative sense. Trust yourself to make good judgments as to whether or not the creativity rolls up its sleeves and goes to work on prospects.

Always remember that when it's time to create winning advertising for your company, you must work openly and closely with those you're expecting to come up with that action-provoking creativity. Give them all the pertinent information you have. If they (and you) need more, go out and get it.

Sure, there are those who shoot from the hip. Those who don't like their creativity "hemmed in" by the realities of the facts. Not me. And not you. For creativity to be on-the-mark, to provoke action, it must be focussed and to a purpose. Does research kill creativity? A while back I answered that question this way:

Does garlic go with strawberry ice cream?
Does the Pope watch "Midnight Blue?"
Does spelunking give you a sunburn?
Does Prince shop at Brooks Brothers?
Does Ivory soap sink?
Does Gloria Steinem consult Phyllis Schafly?
Does Madonna sing Gregorian chants?
Does champagne taste like Milk of Magnesia?
Does Lee Iacocca drive a Honda?
Does Jerry Falwell smoke pot?
Does the IRS believe everything it's told?

Does Tip O'Neill love elephants?
Does Switzerland have a navy?
Does Dolly Parton sleep on her stomach?
Does the Surgeon General inhale?
Does Bill Cosby drink Pepsi?
Does Arafat give to the UJA?
Does Rhett give a damn?

I like to know what to be creative about. I like to know all about the product. The targeted market. The competition. I like to let it all simmer and bubble back in the deep, dark recesses.

And I like the exhilaration of the sudden rush when the sizzling thunderbolt comes from out of nowhere. It's spooky. It's unpredictable. But I know it's always going to come.

As Louis Pasteur put it, in summing up this business of being creative, "Chance favors the prepared mind."

GLOSSARY

Adspeak, Explained.

These basic words and phrases, grouped in their general categories, should help ensure that we're all talking about the same thing be the subject a widow (usually a single word ending a paragraph to make a visually uncomfortable, too short line) or a hitchike (look it up). There are many more terms than these, some quite common and others quite technical and esoteric. But in most cases this fundamental vocabulary will see you through.

Basic Copy Terms

APPEAL: The message of copy that addresses basic needs and concerns, such as health, sexuality, and insecurities.

CAPTION: The explanatory copy under a photograph or illustration.

COPY: The text of a print ad or a radio or TV commercial. It can refer to all the words, including the headline, unless designated specifically as *body copy.*

COPY APPROACH: The manner in which the subject matter of the advertisement is presented.

COPY PLATFORM: The central premise and rationale for the message of the advertising copy.

COPY TEST: Testing the effectiveness and clarity of a piece of copy, using a sampling of the intended audience. The copy is almost always presented in the context of the final ad.

COPYWRITER: The person responsible for creating all the copy elements.

CREDIT LINE: An acknowledgment of photographer, illustrator, or source.

CROSSHEAD: A boldface line centered in a column of text, serving as a heading over different sections of the body copy.

HEADLINE: The isolated word or words leading off the print ad. Usually at the top and usually of larger typesize than the body copy.

LOGO LINE: Sometimes called a *stance line, go-away line,* or *theme line,* it regularly appears with the company or product logo or name. A logo line and slogan are often the same.

REASON WHY: Copy that lays out a logical, objective argument on the benefits and advantages of the product being advertised.

SLOGAN: A phrase that appears consistently in a company's advertising and becomes identified with the product or advertiser.

SUBHEAD: A smaller headline under the main headline.

Basic Art Terms

ANIMATIC: A series of stills, either illustrations or scrap, of what is proposed. It roughly simulates the content and sequence of a commercial.

ANIMATION: This can take any of several forms, but think Walt Disney as apposed to live action, and you've got the idea.

BLOWUP: A photograph, artwork, or printed matter that has been enlarged. For example, a poster-size enlargement of a magazine ad for a meeting or display.

BULLET: A dot used as a paragraph mark to draw attention to a word, phrase, sentence, or group of sentences. Usually used in sets to separate a series of phrases.

BULLPEN: That section of the art department where comps and mechanicals are put together.

CARTOUCHE: A decorative line or frame that gives a special character and appeal to the piece it is part of.

DUMMY: The layout for a booklet or folder, usually bound in the type and weight of the paper to be used, to simulate the feel of the finished piece.

FINISHED COMP: A quite precise simulation of what the final ad will look like. Also called a *tight comp.*

FLUSH: This means the type is aligned vertically either on the left side (*flush left*), or the right side, (*flush right*). The margin opposite the flush is usually *ragged*, that is, left unaligned. Sometimes type is flushed on both sides.

LEADING: The spacing between lines of type. When the lines are too tight, that is, too close together for good reading ability or appearance, the distance between lines can be increased. This is done simply on the computer today, but originally strips of lead were inserted between lines to increase the spacing—thus the terminology.

LETTERING: Hand-drawn letters that represent the approximate look and placement of the intended final typography.

LINE DRAWING: An illustration drawn in line only, usually black line on white background (but the line can be any color, or combinations of color, against any background) without shadings of gray.

MECHANICAL: This is the absolute, final, accurate assembly of all the various elements of an ad or other printed piece, with any instructions as to materials to be stripped in, or whatever, included. It is from this that the film that the printer needs to print your ad or sales piece is made.

MONTAGE: An assembly of a number of photographs, illustrations, and/or graphic elements that make up a single, unified piece of artwork.

MORTISE: A panel or open space in an ad, usually inserted into a photograph, on which text or artwork is placed.

PASTE-UP: Another term for *mechanical.*

RESCALE: An ad can be made smaller or larger to fit another space by *rescaling* or *repositioning.*

RETOUCHING: The altering of a photograph to remove or add something or simply to correct or improve a portion of it, so that it will reproduce to best effect.

ROUGH COMP: The word *comp* is short for *comprehensive,* which just about explains it. A rough comp (or rough layout) is an approximation of the general structure and placement of all the parts of the ad.

SCRAP: Actual torn out photos of art from magazines, newspapers, books, catalogs, or wherever pasted in place on a comp to stand in for what will be the final art in the finished ad.

SILHOUETTE: Think of those old-fashioned cutout profiles that our great-grandparents were so fond of. A silhouette means the outline of a face, body, or object. However, it does not often mean a solid, one-color outline, although it could. Usually it means an outline shape with all the colors and details of the image within it.

THUMBNAILS: Miniature, rough layouts, usually a couple of inches high and usually made with a pencil or Pentel, that depict the general positioning of elements and central idea of a TV or print advertisment or of a printed piece.

TRANSPARENCY: A color film through which light can pass as it does through a negative, but giving a positive image.

TYPOGRAPHY: The style, shapes, and sizes of the words as printed. The most important things to know as regards the creative character and feel of the piece you are working on are the two general classes of type: *serif,* of which the common *Times Roman* is a classic example, with its swirls and thick and thin lines, and *sans serif,* of which *Futura,* with it uniform-width lines and block letters, is a prime example.

VIGNETTE: A photograph or illustration with an edge that is faded gradually into the background so that there is no hard line of separation.

Basic Production Terms

AAs: Less often referred to by this full name—author's alterations. These are changes made in copy already set in type.

BLEED: This means the printed area goes right up to the edge of the paper. When this occurs in a publication, there is often an additional charge for space.

BLIND EMBOSS: A raised impression of letters or artwork in relief only.

BLUE: Short for *blueprint*. A simple reproduction of what a ready-for-printing job looks like as far as positioning, content, etc., for final approval purposes. A *Van Dyke* is a similar print used for the final approval check.

COATED PAPER: Paper that has a smooth, glossy surface. It is particularly suited to fine-screen halftone printing.

DIE CUT: A sheet of paper, usually in a promotion piece, cut in a shape other than a rectangle or square. This includes cutout sections, shortened pages, and so on.

DUOTONE: Printing a photograph in two colors over its entirety at slightly different angles, to give it more depth and richness.

HALFTONE: A photo or artwork that prints in a range of shades. This is a result of the art being broken up into dots, some quite small and spaced apart, others larger, that give the effect of varying gradations of black and white or color.

IMPRINTING: Printing additional copy on a finished printed piece, usually in order to personalize it.

LEADING: The spacing between lines of type. When the lines are too tight, that is, too close together for readability or appearance, the distance between lines can be increased. This is done simply on the computer today, but originally strips of lead were inserted between lines to increase the spacing—thus the terminology.

OFFSET: Short for *offset lithography*. A printing process wherein the image is transferred from the plate to a rubber roller called a *blanket* and thence to the paper.

OUTLINE HALFTONE: Also called a *silhouette halftone,* this is a halftone with its background image cut out, leaving the shape of the art desired.

OVERRUN: A number of printed pieces in excess of the specified quantity. A bonus for the advertiser.

PHOTOSTAT: Most often simply called a *stat.* It is similar to a photograph but is not as finely detailed. It can be made more quickly and cheaply.

POINT SIZE: Or simply *point.* The usual size for type in text is eight-point, nine-point, or ten-point type. There are 72 points to the inch, so a 72-point headline would have letters one inch high.

PROOF: This is, in effect, a test-run printed sheet, run off from the printing press for approval. A last chance to make corrections before a job is printed.

REGISTER: When more than one color is being printed, each color should fall in its exact proper place. If not, it is "out of register."

RESCALE: An ad can be made smaller or larger to fit another space by *rescaling* or *repositioning.*

RETOUCHING: The altering of a photograph to remove or add something or simply to correct or improve a portion of it so that it will reproduce to best effect.

SCREEN: A term referring to the number of dots per inch in a halftone. Coarser newspaper screens might be 55 lines to the inch, whereas some of the finest brochure printing can call for screens of up to 300 lines per inch.

SILK-SCREEN: Essentially this is a stenciling method of printing. It allows for different colors to be printed on a paper or cloth surface, almost always a cover or poster. It can be very graphic and effective but generally makes sense only for a relatively small quantity.

VELOX: This is a photographic print that has been reproduced with halftone dots. Such reproduction allows the art to be shot as line art. Usually this is done to improve newspaper reproduction.

VIGNETTE: A photograph or illustration with an edge that is faded gradually into the background so that there is no hard line of separation.

WEIGHT: An indication of the thickness of the paper to be used for a brochure or other printed piece. For example, in a given job, text paper might be 65 pounds and cover stock might be 100 pounds. This means that five hundred sheets of the text paper in a stated size would weigh 65 pounds, and five hundred sheets of the cover stock would weigh 100 pounds.

Basic Account Management Terms

ACCOUNT EXECUTIVE: The agency contact with the client. The *AE,* as the person is also referred to, coordinates the various areas of the agency to serve the client's needs. Sometimes called *account supervisor* or *account manager,* depending on the nomenclature of the particular agency.

AGENCY CONTRACT: The terms and conditions of the agreement between the agency and the advertiser company. Usually the contract calls for a 90-day winding down period after the agency has been notified that the contract is being terminated. In some cases 60-day or 30-day periods have been agreed to.

CAMPAIGN: A series of ads with a similar appeal, look, and approach.

COMMISSION: Traditionally an agency has received 15 percent of gross media expenditures for creating the advertising and managing its placement. In cases of large budgets, the commission percentage may be negotiated downward by the client. Production costs are usually marked up by 17.65 percent of the net bills to yield the agency 15 percent of the gross amount. In many instances production costs are marked up at a higher percentage.

CONTACT REPORT: Or *status report.* A report issued by the account executive summarizing the content and decisions of a meeting or a substantive phone call. Its purpose is to put these decisions on record; if on receipt of the report there is disagreement about what was agreed to, a resolution should be arrived at before any action is initiated.

FEE: A form of compensation that is becoming considerably more common. A fee may be applied to a project or be structured on a monthly basis. Monthly fees can cover all agency compensation (in which case the agency receives no media or production commissions), be confined to covering just media commissions, be in addition to media commissions, or be part of some such combination, depending on the specific circumstances.

FLOWCHART: Generally this goes hand in glove with the spreadsheet. It is a graphic representation of the dates of print insertions and broadcast times by specific publications, outdoor or poster locations, or radio or TV stations.

MARKETING: A general term referring to the process of manufacturing and selling a product or service, including all steps in between. Some of these steps are competitive research, market research, distribution, and advertising.

MERCHANDISING: This can take two basic forms, depending on the product: 1. It can include various materials announcing an advertising and sales program to dealers, salespeople, customers and prospects, and other groups important to the company. 2. It also refers to promotional displays or literature at the point of purchase.

PRESENTATION: In advertising this usually refers to the showing and telling of facts, arguments, samples of work, or whatever in presenting either a new business solicitation or a proposed campaign to a client.

RELEASE: A signed authorization allowing an agency and the company they represent to use a person's likeness or words on behalf of the advertiser's company or product.

SPREADSHEET: A sheet detailing the budget expenditure by month, week, or day.

Basic Broadcast Media Terms

ACROSS-THE-BOARD: Scheduling a commercial to be broadcast at the same time each day Monday through Friday. Also called a *strip schedule*.

ADI: An *ARB* (American Research Bureau) designation of the geographic area dominantly covered by a local TV or radio station. Also referred to by its full name—Area of Dominant Influence.

AVAIL: Or *availablility.* A time period available to an advertiser.

BILLBOARD: An eight-second to ten-second announcement at the beginning and/or end of a program noting the name of the sponsor.

BOOKING: The formal scheduling of a commercial.

CLEAR TIME: Checking on available time or actually reserving broadcast time with a station or network.

COMMERCIAL IMPRESSIONS: The total audience reached by all commercials in an advertiser's schedule. The number includes duplicate viewings.

CONFIRMATION: An acknowledgment from a station that a requested time period is available to an advertiser.

COVERAGE: A measure of how thoroughly an advertising medium reaches the readers, viewers, or listeners in a particular market.

CPM/PCM: The cost per thousand viewers (or listeners) reached per commercial minute.

CUME: The cumulative audience, as it is also referred to, that a particular TV or radio program will reach, and thus the number of households or people that will be exposed to a commercial on that program.

DAY PARTS: Different segments of a broadcast day, designated as *morning, afternoon, early evening, midevening, late night.* A common further division of the morning and late afternoon day parts is *drive time.*

DOUBLE SPOTTING: Consecutively running two commercials within one commercial time segment. For example, a multiproduct advertiser might divide one time segment in two and feature two different products from its line in turn.

DROP-IN: The insertion of a local commercial into a prerecorded or network television or radio program. Also referred to as a *cut-in.*

FLIGHT: A campaign period, usually a number of weeks, in which the advertising is concentrated. The period between such flights is called a *hiatus.*

FRINGE TIME: Those television time periods just before prime time (*early fringe*) and just after (*late fringe*).

GROSS RATING POINTS: Called *GRPs* for short. This is a numerical rating signifying the percentage of the total potential audience reached.

HITCHHIKE: Running a commercial at the conclusion of a program not being sponsored by the advertiser, thus gaining rub-off identification with the program.

INTEGRATED COMMERCIAL: A commercial that is presented within the framework of the entertainment portion of a television or radio program.

LOCAL RATE: The rate that local advertisers can usually get on their local station, which is lower than that offered to a national advertiser.

MAKE-GOOD: A commercial that is run by a station without additional cost at a time other than when scheduled because it was originally not run when specified, was run incompletely, or was run with interference.

PREEMPTIBLE RATE: An agreed upon lower rate for running a commercial that can be canceled if another advertiser is willing to pay a higher rate.

PRIME TIME: The peak television viewing hours. They are usually mid-evening hours, but they could be at another time, such as during mid-afternoon Super Bowl.

QUINTILE: TV viewers are divided into five equal groups, or quintiles, ranging from the heaviest to the lightest viewers.

REACH: The total possible number of people that can be reached by a specific station, whether or not they have their sets turned on or tuned to that particular station.

ROADBLOCKING: Buying the same time on all stations in a market to insure that the total TV or radio audience at that time is exposed to a specific commercial message.

ROS: This refers to commercials that can be scheduled anytime (*run-of-schedule*) during a period requested by an advertiser. For instance, from noon to 5 P.M. Monday through Friday.

ROTATION: Repeating a series of commercials in a regular, predetermined order.

SCATTER PLAN: Literally commercials that are scattered throughout the broadcast day.

SHARE: Also called *share of audience*. A measurement of the number of sets in use tuned to a specific program, station, or network.

TAG: Usually a retailer identification noting that the product advertised can be bought at their store.

TARGET RATING POINTS: Or *TRPs*. A numerical rating signifying the percentage of the total designated target audience reached.

TOTAL AUDIENCE: The number of individual viewers tuned to a program for at least six minutes.

TPR: A time period rating—a general rating for a particular time period without considering what specific program is being broadcast. For example, the TPR for 8:00 P.M. is universally much higher than for 4:00 A.M.

VERTICAL CUME: A measure of the total audience reached in successive programs.

VERTICAL SATURATION: Reaching as many people as possible in as short a time period as possible, by scheduling a great many commercials throughout the day for one or several days.

Basic Print Media Terms

AGATE LINE: A unit of newspaper space 1/14 of an inch deep by one column wide.

AVERAGE NET PAID CIRCULATION: The average number of copies that a magazine or newspaper sells per issue.

CENTER SPREAD: An ad printed on a single sheet making up the left- and right-hand pages in the center of a publication.

CHECKING COPY: A copy of the issue including an advertiser's ad, sent by the publication to prove that the ad appeared as requested.

CIRCULATION: The total number of copies of a publication distributed per issue. Note that all copies distributed may not have been sold.

CLASSIFIED: Paid-for notices appearing in a newspaper or magazine. Usually separated into special categories, such as real estate, automobiles, and so on. Set in small type and usually quite direct in its information and offer. *Display classified* appears generally in larger space and often employs some of the elements of display advertising.

CLOSING DATE: The deadline for material to be delivered to a publication if it is to appear in a specific issue. In some cases a day or more extension may be granted.

COLUMN INCH: Magazine or newspaper space one inch in depth by one column wide.

COMBO RATE: A discounted combination rate for advertising in two or more publications owned by the same publishing company.

CONTROLLED CIRCULATION: This refers to copies sent to a certain qualifying group of readers who receive the publication free of charge. The purpose is to insure a broad coverage of a desirable market in order to attract advertisers appropiate to that market.

CO-OP: Usually retail advertising paid for wholly or in part by the manufacturer of a product or products sold through the retail outlet. The amount of manufacturer participation is generally dependent upon the amount of merchandise ordered.

CPM: Cost per thousand. The cost of creating and presenting an advertisement to one thousand readers.

DISPLAY ADVERTISING: Advertising utilizing one or more of the following: typography, photography, or illustration. From the smallest-size units to full pages, spreads, and multiple pages.

FACING TEXT: A desirable situation in which the ad is opposite editorial material. Note that there can be a higher charge for this position.

FIXED LOCATION: The same position in a publication (for example, inside front cover or outside column on page 7) in each issue the advertisement appears in.

GUTTER: The center vertical crease between pages in a publication.

ISLAND POSITION: This refers to either a print ad surrounded by editorial matter or a television or radio commercial preceded and followed by program content.

JUNIOR PAGE: Or *junior unit.* A print ad prepared for a smaller-formatted publication that is run in a larger-formatted publication with editorial matter taking up the extra space. An ad can, of course, be orginally designed as a junior page for a larger-size publication.

MAKE-GOOD: An advertisement that is rerun by the publisher of a magazine or newspaper because the original insertion was incorrectly run or the reproduction was faulty.

PASS-ALONG READERS: Those readers who did not buy the original copy of a publication but who read it. General magazines usually have three to four readers per copy.

PRIMARY READERS: The subscribers or newsstand buyers of a publication.

PUBLISHER'S STATEMENT: The circulation figure, geographic distribution, etc. attested to by the publisher of a magazine or newspaper.

RATE CARD: A listing of the various rates for a particular publication, discussing different sized ads, color vs. black-and-white ads, specific positions, frequency discounts, and so on.

REACH: The total number of people that a specific publication covers, whether or not they ever pick it up.

ROP: Or *run-of-paper.* This means that an advertisement can appear in any part of the publication at the publisher's discretion.

SAUs: Or *standard advertising units*. Units of space, used for measuring purposes by most daily newspapers. All told, there are 56 different broadsheet advertising unit sizes and 33 tabloid advertising unit sizes.

TRIM SIZE: The measurement of a magazine page after it has been trimmed in putting together the magazine. A little extra space in the mechanical is allowed for because of this trimming.

VERTICAL PUBLICATION: A magazine or paper that covers a specific industry or trade group.

WASTE CIRCULATION: This can mean that part of the circulation of a publication is in a geographic area where an advertised product is not distributed. It also can refer to those readers who are not potential customers for a featured product or service such as the male portion of an audience exposed to a lipstick ad.

Basic Outdoor And Transit Terms

BILLBOARD: The structure that holds an outdoor advertisement. The ad itself can be painted onto the board or have printed sheets glued onto it.

EFFECTIVE CIRCULATION: This is a reasonable estimate (as defined by the Traffic Audit Bureau) of the number of people passing an out-of-home ad, on foot or in a vehicle, who might reasonably be assumed to have seen the ad.

FULL RUN: Or *full showing*. The number of outdoor postings needed to reach a specific market's entire mobile population at least once within a 30 day period.

GROSS CIRCULATION: The total number of people passing an outdoor ad, whether facing it or not during a specific period of time.

INDIVIDUAL LOCATION: An outdoor location that is only able to accommodate one billboard.

ONE-SHEET POSTER: A single sheet, either 30 inches by 46 inches or 28 inches by 42 inches, usually appearing in bus, train, or subway stations.

PAINTED BULLETIN: A billboard that is hand-painted in grids, following a guide of the desired finished advertisment.

POSTER PANEL: A billboard onto which printed paper sheets are posted. The standard dimensions for a poster billboard are 25 feet in width by 12 feet in height. Usually it takes between 10 to 30 printed sheets to fill the face of the board.

POSTING: The act of actually putting up the advertisment (by posting printed sheets or painting by hand) on the billboard or poster locations.

POSTING PERIOD: The length of time contracted for in displaying the advertisement. The usual period is 30 days.

SHOWING: The number of outdoor ads or transit ads that are part of a package buy.

SPACE POSITION VALUE: The desirability and effectiveness of an outdoor advertising location. Considerations determining space position value would include how far the board or poster can be seen, the number and speed of passing cars and the amount of pedestrian traffic, how many if any competing boards or posters are near it, its height and angle, and so on.

SPECTACULAR: A major, lighted outdoor billboard.

Basic Research Terms

AIDED RECALL: A test in which the question asked is in the form of a prompt. It usually includes a direct query on whether the respondent remembers seeing a commercial or a print ad for a particular product (or group of products) and a request that the respondent describe the key point in his or her own words.

ASI: A testing service that transmits commercials and prototype programs being tested to participating homes over a special TV channel. Attitudinal questions are asked via telephone the next day.

ATTRIBUTE: The inherent character of a product or service. For example, sturdily made (furniture), very spicy (food), courteous (flight attendants).

AWARE NON-TRIER: A prospect for a product who is aware of the product but has not personally experienced it to date.

BLIND PRODUCT TEST: A comparison test of competitive products in which the brand names are removed.

BUFFER QUESTION: A nonrelevant question inserted between important questions in a reasearch study. Its purpose is to distract or break up the rhythm of the questioning in an interview.

BURKE: A reasearch company that devised widely used percentage score measurement to suggest the effectiveness of a given TV commercial. The technique involved a telephone survey the day after the showing of a commercial. This service was discontinued in mid-1990.

CLOSE-END QUESTION: The response to the question is limited to a choice presented within the question. Either-or and multiple-choice.

CONCEPT TEST: Literally the testing of a concept, as opposed to the testing of an actual product. This could include the idea of an ad or commercial, a new product, a proposed package design, and so forth.

CONSUMER PANEL: A group of people respresenting a cross section of a market who are asked their opinion of an advertising campaign, specific products, or whatever.

COPY-POINT RECALL: How much and what of an advertisement is acurately remembered and understood.

CROSS TAB: Cross-referencing and separating the answers to a research study by groups. For example, if 80 percent of all respondents said yes, they regularly use a product, the cross tabulations may indicate how many are women, how many went to college, how many have incomes over $25,000, or some such information appropriate and useful to the needs of marketing.

DEMOGRAPHICS: The basic profile of any particular group, including fundamental data such as gender, age, income and accumulated wealth, ethnic and/or religious background, levels of education, travel habits, car and home ownerships, etc,

DIAGNOSTIC RESEARCH: This differs from research that compares a product against a benchmark set of numbers or comparative data.

Diagnostic research focuses on the psychological reasons something is working or not working.

FIELD: Where the research involving consumers in real-life situations is taking place. Mall intercepts (stopping a shopper in or outside a store and asking questions) are a quite common technique. Also refers collectively to the people and their supervisors who do the actual surveying.

FOCUS GROUP: Also referred to as a *group session.* A professional leader asks questions of a half-dozen or so specified consumer types (cola drinkers, working mothers, or whomever) seated around a table. The concept is that a group discussion evokes more open answers and offers good insights into how consumers may be relating to a product.

IN-DEPTH INTERVIEW: A one-on-one, probing interview to elicit responses that indicate how the respondent really feels about a product. The technique used to elicit meaningful responses calls for a well-trained person with the skill to get and keep the respondent on track, and an ability to press for clarifications to learn exactly what goes on in the respondent subconscious when they see or hear the name of a specific product.

INDEX: A term referring to the numerical value given quantitative data for comparative measurement purposes.

INTERCEPT: The process of stopping people for an interview at a specific location, such as a shopping mall.

KEYING: A process by which a separate code—usually appearing on a coupon or as part of a return address—is used for each different medium carrying an ad, so that the responses can be attributed to the proper carrier.

MARKET POTENTIAL: That share of the market that a product can reasonably be expected to achieve.

MARKET PROFILE: A general description of the competition, the economy, the demographic characteristics of all those who are reasonable prospects for a particular product, and other characteristics of a market.

MARKET SHARE: The amount of sales won by a product, compared to the sales of other brands of the same specific type.

NET UNDUPLICATED AUDIENCE: The total number of people reached by one issue of two or more publications.

NIELSEN: A rating service that measures the popularity of various television programs.

OPEN-END QUESTION: The respondent is free to answer the question in any words and in any way he or she chooses. The answers have to be coded in a manner that can then be tabulated.

PORTFOLIO TEST: A booklet containing a number of ads for a respondent to look through. After viewing them, questions are asked relating to the specific ads just seen.

PRE-POST: A testing procedure in which a number of things are tested both prior to and immediately after an advertising program to determine the effectiveness of a campaign.

PRE-TEST: Generally refers to testing a commercial or print ad before it is placed in paid media.

THE PRETESTING COMPANY: A reasearch service that scientifically uses patented technologies to measure the switching of stations to avoid TV commercials, patterns of print ad examination and readership, and on-shelf packaging performance.

PROBABILITY SAMPLE: A group of persons chosen for testing purposes for which all possible individuals in a specified group have an equal chance of being chosen as respondents.

QUINTILE: TV viewers are divided into five equal groups, or quintiles, ranging from the heaviest to the lightest viewers.

SCREENING: A process whereby respondents who do not qualify (for example, those who never use after-shave or cologne) are weeded out at the outset or early on in a research study.

SHARE: Also called *share of audience*. A measurement of the number of sets in use tuned to a specific program, station, or network.

SPLIT RUN: Testing two or more versions of an advertisement, by running them in equal numbers of a single issue of a publication.

STARCH: A research technique named after its originator, Daniel Starch, that exposes a current or recent issue of a magazine to a respondent and determines whether he or she remembers seeing the ad, reading the ad in whole or part, and whether he or she can associate it with a product or company. The results are weighted against the cost of the ad to determine its ultimate efficiency.

TEST CAMPAIGN: Testing an advertising idea in a narrow, local market before going to a broader audience. Essentially putting your big toe in the water before going all the way.

UNAIDED RECALL: A test of which brand names are uppermost in a respondent's mind. For example, a typical unaided recall question might ask, "Consider the product category dandruff shampoo— which brand names do you immediately think of?"

VERTICAL CUME: A measure of the total audience reached in two or more programs broadcast on the same day.

Alphabetical Glossary

AAs: Less often referred to by their full name—author's alterations. These are changes made in copy already set in type.

ACCOUNT EXECUTIVE: The agency contact with the client. The *AE*, as the person is also referred to, coordinates the various areas of the agency to serve the client's needs. Sometimes called *account supervisor* or *account manager*, depending on the nomenclature of the particular agency.

ACROSS-THE-BOARD: Scheduling a commercial to be broadcast at the same time each day Monday through Friday. Also called a *strip schedule.*

ADI: An *ARB* (American Research Bureau) designation of the geographic area dominantly covered by a local TV or radio station. Also referred to by its full name—Area of Dominant Influence.

AGATE LINE: A unit of newspaper space 1/14 of an inch deep by one column wide.

AGENCY CONTRACT: The terms and conditions of the agreement between the agency and the advertiser company. Usually the contract calls for a 90-day winding down period after the agency has been notified that the contract is being terminated. In some cases 60-day or 30-day periods have been agreed to.

AIDED RECALL: A test in which the question asked is in the form of a prompt. It usually includes a direct query on whether the respondent remembers seeing a commercial or a print ad for a particular product (or group of products) and a request that the respondent describe the key point in his or her own words.

ANIMATIC: A series of stills, either illustrations or scrap, of what is proposed. It roughly simulates the content and sequence of a commercial.

ANIMATION: This can take any of several forms; but think Walt Disney as opposed to live action, and you've got the idea.

APPEAL: The message of copy that addresses basic needs and concerns, such as one's health, sexuality, and insecurities.

ASI: A testing service that transmits commercials and prototype programs being tested to participating homes over a special TV channel. Attitudinal questions are asked via telephone the next day.

ATTRIBUTE: The inherent character of a product or service. For example, sturdily made (furniture), very spicy (food), courteous (flight attendants).

AVAIL: Or *availability*. A time period available to an advertiser.

AVERAGE NET PAID CIRCULATION: The average number of copies that a magazine or newspaper sells per issue.

AWARE NON-TRIER: A prospect for a product who is aware of the product but has not personally experienced it to date.

BARTER: Usually used in reference to an advertising medium offering its space or time in exchange for merchandise or some type of consideration other than cash.

BILLBOARD: 1. An eight-second to ten-second announcement at the beginning and/or end of a program noting the name of the sponsor. 2. The structure that holds an outdoor advertisement. The ad itself can be painted onto the board or have printed sheets glued onto it.

BLEED: This means the printed area goes right up to the edge of the paper. When this occurs in a publication, there is often an additional charge for space.

BLIND EMBOSS: A raised impression of letters or artwork in relief only.

BLIND PRODUCT TEST: A comparison test of competitive products in which the brand names are removed.

BLOWUP: A photograph, artwork, or printed matter that has been enlarged. For example, a poster-size enlargement of a magazine ad for a meeting or display.

BLUE: Short for *blueprint*. A simple reproduction of what a ready-for-printing job looks like as far as positioning, content, etc., for final approval purposes. A *Van Dyke* is a similar print used for the final approval check.

BOOKING: The formal scheduling of a commercial.

BROADSHEET: Standard newspaper size (generally 13 inches by 21 inches), as opposed to tabloid size (approximately 10 inches by 13 inches).

BROADSIDE: An announcement or offer usually printed on one side of a sheet of paper.

BUFFER QUESTION: A nonrelevant question inserted between important questions in a research study. Its purpose is to distract or break up the rhythm of the questioning in an interview.

BULLET: A dot used as a paragraph mark to draw attention to a word, phrase, sentence, or group of sentences. Usually used in sets to separate a series of phrases.

BULLPEN: That section of the art department where comps and mechanicals are put together.

BURKE: A reasearch company that devised widely used percentage score measurement to suggest the effectiveness of a given TV commercial. The technique involved a telephone survey the day after the showing of a commercial. This service was discontinued in mid-1990.

BUYING SERVICE: A specialized company that performs those functions traditionally performed by an advertising agency's media department.

CAMPAIGN: A series of ads with a similar appeal or look, and approach.

CAPTION: The explanatory copy under a photograph or illustration.

CARTOUCHE: A decorative line or frame that gives a special character and appeal to the piece it is part of.

CENTER SPREAD: An ad printed on a single sheet making up the left- and righ-hand pages in the center of a publication.

CHECKING COPY: A copy of the issue including an advertiser's ad, sent by the publication to prove that the ad appeared as requested.

CIRCULATION: The total number of copies of a publication distributed per issue. Note that all copies distributed may not have been sold.

CLASSIFIED: Paid-for notices appearing in a newspaper or magazine. Usually separated into special categories, such as real estate, automobiles, and so on. Set in small type and usually quite direct in their information and offer. *Display classified* appears generally in larger space and often employs some of the elements of display advertising.

CLEAR TIME: Checking on available time or actually reserving broadcast time with a station or network.

CLOSED-END QUESTION: The response to the question is limited to a choice presented within the question. Either/or and multiple-choice.

CLOSING DATE: The deadline for material to be delivered to a publication if it is to appear in a specific issue. In some cases a day or more extension may be granted.

COATED PAPER: Paper that has a smooth, glossy surface. It is particularly suited to fine-screen halftone printing.

COLUMN INCH: Magazine or newspaper space one inch in depth by one column wide.

COMBO RATE: A discounted combination rate for advertising in two or more publications owned by the same publishing company.

COMMERCIAL IMPRESSIONS: The total audience reached by all commercials in an advertiser's schedule. The number includes duplicate viewings.

COMMISSION: Traditionally an agency has received 15 percent of gross media expenditures for creating the advertising and managing its placement. In cases of large budgets, the commission percentage may be negotiated downward by the client. Production costs are usually marked up by 17.65 percent of the net bills to yield the agency 15 percent of the gross amount. In many instances production costs are marked up at a higher percentage.

CONCEPT TEST: Literally the testing of a concept, as opposed to the testing of an actual product. This could include the idea of an ad or commercial, a new product, a proposed package design, and so forth.

CONFIRMATION: An acknowledgment from a station that a requested time period is available to an advertiser.

CONSUMER PANEL: A group of people representing a cross section of a market who are asked their opinion of an advertising campaign, specific products, or whatever.

CONTACT REPORT: Or *status report*. A report issued by the account executive summarizing the content and decisions of a meeting or a substantive phone call. Its purpose is to put these decisions on record; if on receipt of the report there is disagreement about what was agreed to, a resolution should be arrived at before any action is initiated.

CONTROLLED CIRCULATION: This refers to copies sent to a certain qualifying group of readers who receive the publication free of charge. The purpose is to insure a broad coverage of a desirable market in order to attract advertisers appropriate to that market.

CO-OP: Usually retail advertising paid for wholly or in part by the manufacturer of a product or products sold through the retail outlet. The amount of manufacturer participation is generally dependent upon the amount of merchandise ordered.

COPY: The text of a print ad or a radio or TV commercial. It can refer to all the words, including the headline, unless designated specifically as *body copy*.

COPY APPROACH: The manner in which the subject matter of the advertisement is presented.

COPY PLATFORM: the central premise and rationale for the message of the advertising copy.

COPY-POINT RECALL: How much and what of an advertisement is accurately remembered and understood.

COPY TEST: Testing the effectiveness and clarity of a piece of copy, using a sampling of the intended audience. The copy is almost always presented in the context of the final ad.

COPYWRITER: The person responsible for creating all the copy elements.

COVERAGE: A measure of how thoroughly an advertising medium reaches the readers, viewers, or listeners in a particular market.

CPM: Cost per thousand. The cost of creating and presenting an advertisement to one thousand readers.

CPM/PCM: The cost per thousand viewers (or listeners) reached per commercial minute.

CREDIT LINE: An acknowledgment of photographer, illustrator, or source.

CROPPING: Cutting off part of a photograph, illustration, or other element of the layout.

CROSSHEAD: A boldface line centered in a column of text, serving as a heading over different sections of the body copy.

CROSS TAB: Cross-referencing and separating the answers to a research study by groups. For example, if 80 percent of all respondents said yes, they regularly use a product, the cross tabulations may indicate how many are women, how many went to college, how many have incomes over $25,000, or some such information appropriate and useful to the needs of marketing.

CUME: The cumulative audience, as it is also referred to, that a particular TV or radio program will reach, and thus the number of households or people that will be exposed to a commercial on that program.

CUT-IN: The insertion of a local commercial into a prerecorded or network television or radio program. Also referred to as a *drop-in.*

DAY PARTS: Different segments of a broadcast day, designated as *morning, afternoon, early evening, midevening, late night.* A common further division of the morning and late afternoon day parts is *drive time.*

DEMOGRAPHICS: The basic profile of any particular group, including fundamental data such as gender, age, income and accumulated wealth, ethnic and/or religious background, levels of education, travel habits, car and home ownership, etc.

DIAGNOSTIC RESEARCH: This differs from research that compares a product against a benchmark set of numbers or comparative data. Diagnostic research focuses on the psychological reasons for *why* something is working or not working.

DIE CUT: A sheet of paper, usually in a promotion piece, cut in a shape other than a rectangle or square. This includes cutout sections, shortened pages, and so on.

DIRECT ADVERTISING: Advertising that is distributed to prospects either door-to-door, through the mails, stuffed into grocery bags, or in some other manner.

DIRECT MAIL ADVERTISING: Any sort of promotional material sent directly to possible purchasers through the mails.

DISPLAY: This term applies almost always to in-store materials such as posters, aisle enders, window displays, and the like that promote a product.

DISPLAY ADVERTISING: Advertising utilizing one or more of the following: typography, photography, or illustration. From the smallest-size units to full pages, spreads, and multiple pages.

DOUBLE SPOTTING: Consecutively running two commercials within one commercial time segment. For example, a multiproduct advertiser might divide one time segment in two and feature two different products from its line in turn.

DROP-IN: The insertion of a local commercial into a prerecorded or network television or radio program. Also referred to as a *cut-in*.

DUMMY: The layout for a booklet or folder, usually bound in the type and weight of the paper to be used, to simulate the feel of the finished piece.

DUOTONE: Printing a photograph in two colors over its entirety at slightly different angles, to give it more depth and richness.

EFFECTIVE CIRCULATION: This is a reasonable estimate (as defined by the Traffic Audit Bureau) of the number of people passing an out-of-home ad, on foot or in a vehicle, who might reasonably be assumed to have seen the ad.

FACING TEXT: A desirable situation in which the ad is opposite editorial material. Note that there can be a higher charge for this position.

FEE: A form of compensation that is becoming considerably more common. A fee may be applied to a project or be structured on a monthly basis. Monthly fees can cover all agency compensation (in which case the agency receives no media or production commissions), be confined to covering just media commissions, be in addition to media commissions,or be part of some such combination, depending on the specific circumstances.

FIELD: Where the research involving consumers in real-life situations is taking place. Mall intercepts (stopping a shopper in or outside a store and asking questions) are a quite common technique. Also refers collectively to the people and their supervisors who do the actual surveying.

FILL-IN: On a letter, a recipient's name and address that has been filled in to appear individually typed.

FINISHED COMP: A quite precise simulation of what the final ad will look like. Also called a *tight comp.*

FIXED LOCATION: The same position in a publication (for example, inside front cover or outside column on page 7) in each issue the advertisement appears in.

FLIGHT: A campaign period, usually a number of weeks, in which the advertising is concentrated. The period between such flights is called a *hiatus*.

FLOWCHART: Generally this goes hand in glove with the spread-sheet. It is a graphic representation of the dates of print insertions and broadcast times by specific publications, outdoor or poster locations, or radio or TV stations.

FLUSH: This means the type is aligned vertically either on the left side (*flush left*), or the right side, (*flush right*). The margin opposite the flush side is usually *ragged*, that is, left unaligned. Somtimes type is flushed on both sides.

FOCUS GROUP: Also referred to as a *group session*. A professional leader asks questions of a half-dozen or so specified consumer types (cola drinkers, working mothers, or whomever) seated around a table. The concept is that a group discussion evokes more open answers and offers good insights into how consumers may be relating to a product.

FREE LANCE: More often than not this refers to a copywriter, art director, or mechical artist not on staff who works on individual assignments for an hourly, daily, or project fee.

FREE-STANDING INSERT: Often called simply an *FSI*. A section or a single page prepared by an advertiser that is inserted within the newspaper.

FREQUENCY DISCOUNT: A discount given by an advertising medi-um for specified numbers of ads run within a year or other time period.

FRINGE TIME: Those television time periods just before prime time (*early fringe*) and just after (*late fringe*).

FULL RUN: Or *full showing*. The number of outdoor postings needed to reach a specific market's entire mobile population at least once within a given 30 day period.

GROSS CIRCULATION: The total number of people passing an outdoor ad, whether facing it or not, during a specific period of time.

GROSS RATING POINTS: Called *GRPs* for short. This is a numerical rating signifying the percentage of the total potential audience reached.

GUTTER: The center vertical crease between pages in a publication.

HALFTONE: A photo or artwork that prints in a range of shades. This is a result of the art being broken up into dots, some quite small and spaced apart, others larger, that give the effect of varying gradations of black and white or color.

HEADLINE: The isolated word or words leading off the print ad. Usually at the top and usually of larger type size than the body copy.

HITCHHIKE: Running a commercial at the conclusion of a program not being sponsored by the advertiser, thus gaining rub-off identification with the program.

HOUSE AGENCY: A group within a company that performs much the same functions as an outside, independent advertising agency.

IMPRINTING: Printing additional copy on a finished printed piece, usually in order to personalize it.

IN-DEPTH INTERVIEW: A one-on-one, probing interview to elicit responses that indicate how the respondent really feels about a product. The technique used to elicit meaningful responses calls for well-trained person with the skill to get and keep the respondent on track, and an ability to press for clarifications to learn exactly what goes on in the respondent subconscious when they see or hear the name of a specific product.

INDEX: A term referring to the numerical value given quantitative data for comparative measurement purposes.

INDIVIDUAL LOCATION: An outdoor location that is only able to accommodate one billboard.

INTEGRATED COMMERCIAL: A commercial that is presented within the framework of the entertainment portion of a television or radio program.

INTERCEPT: The process of stopping people for an interview at a specific location, such as a shopping mall.

ISLAND POSITION: This refers to either a print ad surrounded by editorial matter or a television or radio commercial preceded and followed by program content.

JUNIOR PAGE: Or *junior unit.* A print ad prepared for a smaller-formatted publication that is run in a larger-formatted publication, with editorial matter taking up the extra space. An ad can, of course, be originally designed as a junior page for a larger-size publication.

KEYING: A process by which a separate code—usually appearing on a coupon or as part of a return address—is used for each different medium carrying an ad, so that the responses can be attrributed to the proper carrier.

LEADING: The spacing between lines of type. When the lines are too tight, that is, too close together for good readability or appearance, the distance between lines can be increased. This is done simply on the computer today, but originally strips of lead were inserted between lines to increase the spacing—thus the terminology.

LETTERING: Hand-drawn letters that represent the approximate look and placement of the intended final typography.

LINE DRAWING: An illustration drawn in line only, usually black line on white background (but the line can be any color, or combinations of color, against any background) without shadings of gray.

LOCAL RATE: The rate that local advertisers can usually get on their local station, which is lower than that offered to a national advertiser.

LOGO LINE: Sometimes called a *stance line, go–away line,* or *theme line,* it regularly appears with the company or product logo or name. A logo line and slogan are often the same.

MAIL ORDER: The business advertises to a market, the customer requests the product, and the business ships the product to the respondent, all entirely through the mails.

MAKE-GOOD: 1. A commercial that is run by a station without additional cost at a time other than when scheduled because it was originally not run when specified, was run imcompletely, or was run with interference.
2. An advertisement that is rerun by the publisher of a magazine or

newspaper because the original insertion was incorrectly run or the reproduction was faulty.

MARKET POTENTIAL: That share of the market that a product can be reasonably be expected to achieve.

MARKET PROFILE: A general description of the competition, the economy, the demographic characteristics of all those who are reasonable prospects for a particular product, and other characteristics of a market.

MARKET SHARE: The amount of sales won by a product, compared to the sales of other brands of the same specific type.

MARKETING: A general term referring to the process of manufacturing and selling a product or service, including all steps in between. Some of these steps are competitive research, market research, distribution, and advertising.

MECHANICAL: This is the absolute, final, accurate assembly of all instructions as to materials to be stripped in, or whatever, included. It is from this that the film that the printer needs to print your ad or sales piece is made.

MEDIA BUYER: The person responsible for buying advertising space or time.

MEDIA PLANNER: The person responsible for choosing the most effective medium or combination of mediums to reach the target market for the product to be advertised.

MERCHANDISING: This can take two basic forms, depending on the product:
1. It can include various materials announcing an advertising and sales program to dealers, salespeople, customers and prospects, and other groups important to the company.
2. It also refers to promotional displays or literature at the point of purchase.

MONTAGE: An assembly of a number of photographs, illustrations, and/or graphic elements that make up a single, unified piece of artwork.

MORTISE: A panel or open space in an ad, usually inserted into a photograph, on which text or artwork is placed.

NET UNDUPLICATED AUDIENCE: The total number of people reached by one issue of two or more publications.

NEXT TO READING MATTER: The placement of a print ad next to editorial matter. Usually a premium position.

NIELSEN: A rating service that measures the popularity of various television programs.

OFFSET: Short for *offset lithography.* A printing process wherein the image is transferred from the plate to a rubber roller called a *blanket* and thence to the paper.

ONE-SHEET POSTER: A single sheet, either 30 inches by 46 inches or 28 inches by 42 inches, usually appearing in bus, train, or subway stations.

OPEN-END QUESTION: The respondent is free to answer the question in any words and in any way he or she chooses. The answers have to be coded in a manner that can then be tabulated.

OUTLINE HALFTONE: Also called a *silhouette halftone,* this is a halftone with its background image cut out, leaving the shape of the art desired.

OVERRUN: A number of printed pieces in excess of the specified quantity. A bonus for the advertiser.

PAINTED BULLETIN: A billboard that is hand-painted in grids, following a guide of the desired finished advertisement.

PASS-ALONG READERS: Those readers who did not buy the original copy of a publication but who read it. General magazines usually have three to four readers per copy.

PASTE-UP: Another term for *mechanical.*

PHOTOSTAT: Most often simply called a *stat.* It is similar to a photograph but is not as finely detailed. It can be made more quickly and cheaply.

POINT SIZE: Or simply *point*. The usual size for type in text is eight-point, nine-point, or ten-point type. There are 72 points to the inch, so a 72-point headline would have letters one inch high.

PORTFOLIO TEST: A booklet containing a number of ads for a respondent to look through. After viewing them, questions are asked relating to the specific ads just seen.

POSTER PANEL: A billboard onto which printed paper sheets are posted. The standard dimensions for a poster billboard are 25 feet by 12 feet in height. Usually it takes between 10 to 30 printed sheets to fill the face of the board.

POSTING: The act of actually putting up the advertisement (by pasting printed sheets or painting by hand) on the billboard or poster locations.

POSTING PERIOD: The length of time contracted for in displaying the advertisement. The usual period is 30 days.

PREEMPTIBLE RATE: An agreed-upon lower rate for running a commercial that can be canceled if another advertiser is willing to pay a higher rate.

PREMIUM: The offer of some sort of merchandise as a free bonus or for a token price, to encourage the purchase of a product.

PRE-POST: A testing procedure in which a number of things are tested both prior to and immediately after an advertising program to determine the effectiveness of a campaign.

PRESENTATION: In advertising this usually refers to the showing and telling of facts, arguments, samples of work, or whatever in presenting either a new business solicitation or a proposed campaign to a client.

PRE-TEST: Generally refers to testing a commercial or print ad before it is placed in paid media.

THE PRETESTING COMPANY: A research service that scientifically uses patented technologies to measure the switching of stations to avoid TV commercials, patterns of print ad examination and readership, and on-shelf packaging performance.

PRIMARY READERS: The subscribers or newsstand buyers of a publication.

PRIME TIME: The peak television viewing hours. They are usually mid-evening hours, but they could be at another time, such as during a mid-afternoon Super Bowl.

PROBABILITY SAMPLE: A group of persons chosen for testing purposes for which all possible individuals in a specified group have an equal chance of being chosen as respondents.

PRODUCT PROTECTION: The separation by time between competing product commercials aired on television or radio.

PROMOTION: Advertising materials other than the advertising placed in paid print or broadcast media.

PROOF: This is, in effect, a test-run printed sheet, run off from the printing press for approval. A last chance to make corrections before a job is printed.

PUBLISHER'S STATEMENT: The circulation figure, geographic distribution, etc. attested to by the publisher of a magazine or newspaper.

QUINTILE: TV viewers are divided into five equal groups, or quintiles, ranging from the heaviest to the lightest viewers.

RATE CARD: A listing of the various rates for a particular publication, discussing different sized ads, color vs. black-and-white ads, specific positions, frequency discounts, and so on.

REACH: 1. The total possible number of people that can be reached by a specific station, whether or not they have their sets turned on or tuned to that particular station.
2. The total number of people that a specific publication covers, whether or not they ever pick it up.

REASON-WHY: Copy that lays out a logical, objective argument on the benefits and advantages of the product being advertised.

RED BOOK: The colloquial name for the *Standard Directory of Advertisers*, which lists advertisers by industry, and the *Standard Directory of Advertising Agencies*, which lists agencies.

REGISTER: When more than one color is being printed, each color should fall in its exact proper place. If not, it is "out of register."

RELEASE: A signed authorization allowing an agency and the company they represent to use a person's likeness or words on behalf of the advertiser's company or product.

RESCALE: An ad can be made smaller or larger to fit another space by *rescaling* or *repositioning.*

RETOUCHING: The altering of a photograph to remove or add something or simply to correct or improve a portion of it, so that it will reproduce to best effect.

ROADBLOCKING: Buying the same time on all stations in a market to insure that the total TV or radio audience at that time is exposed to a specific commercial message.

ROP: Or *run-of-paper.* This means that an advertisement can appear in any part of the publication at the publisher's discretion.

ROS: This refers to commercials that can be scheduled anytime (*run-of-schedule*) during a period requested by an advertiser. For instance, from noon to 5:00 P.M. Monday through Friday.

ROTATION: Repeating a series of commercials in a regular, predetermined order.

ROUGH COMP: The word *comp* is short for *comprehensive,* which just about explains it. A rough comp (or rough layout) is an approximation of the general structure and placement of all the parts of the ad.

ROUGH CUT: An assemblage of the sequences of a commercial to approximate what the final, edited, finished commercial might look like.

SAMPLING: Distributing free samples of a product, with the hope that those trying it will soon be buying it.

SAUS: Or *standard advertising units.* Units of space, used for measuring purposes by most daily newspapers. All told, there are 56 different broadsheet advertising unit sizes and 33 tabloid advertising unit sizes.

SCATTER PLAN: Literally commercials that are scattered throughout the broadcast day.

SCRAP: Actual torn out photos of art from magazines, newspapers, books, catalogs, or wherever pasted in place on a comp to stand in for what will be the final art in the finished ad.

SCREEN: A term referring to the number of dots per inch in a halftone. Coarser newspaper screens might be 55 lines to the inch, whereas some of the finest borchure printing can call for screens of up to 300 lines per inch.

SCREENING: 1. A process whereby respondents who do not qualify (for example, those who never use after-shave or cologne) are weeded out at the outset or early on in a research study.
2. The showing of a finsihed commercial or rough cut.

SELF-MAILER: A return-mail piece that can be sealed, has a place for the address and the stamp or is already addressed and stamped, and needs no envelope.

SHARE: Also called *share of audience.* A measurment of the number of sets in use tuned to a specific program, station, or network.

SHOWING: The number of outdoor ads or transit ads that are part of a package buy.

SILHOUETTE: Think of those old-fashioned cutout profiles that our great-grandparents were so fond of. A silhouette means the outline of a face, body, or object. However, it does not often mean a solid, one-color outline, although it could. Usually it means an outline shape with all the colors and details of the image within it.

SILK-SCREEN: Essentially this is a stenciling method of printing. It allows for different colors to be printed on a paper or cloth surface, almost always a cover or poster. It can be very graphic and effective but generally makes sense only for a relatively small quantity.

SLICE OF LIFE: A television commercial that simulates a real life situation, usually featuring the product being used or being talked about. Also referred to simply as *slice.*

SLOGAN: A phrase that appears consistently in a company's advertising and becomes identified with the product or advertiser.

SPACE POSITION VALUE: The desirability and effectiveness of an outdoor advertising location. Considerations determining space position value would include how far the board or poster can be seen, the number and speed of passing cars and the amount of pedestrian traffic, how many if any competing boards or posters are near it, its height and angle, and so on.

SPECTACTULAR: A major, lighted outdoor billboard.

SPLIT RUN: Testing two or more versions of an advertisement, by running them in equal numbers of a single issue of a publication.

SPREADSHEET: A sheet detailing the budget expenditure by month, week, or day.

STARCH: A research technique named after its originator, Daniel Starch, that exposes a current or recent issue of a magazine to a respondent and determines whether he or she remembers seeing the ad, reading the ad in whole or part, and whether he or she can associate it with a product or company. The results are weighted against the cost of the ad to determine its ultimate efficiency.

SUBHEAD: A smaller headline under the main headline.

TAG: Usually a retailer identification noting that the product advertised can be bought at their store.

TARGET RATING POINTS: Or *TRPs*. A numerical rating signifying the percentage of the total designated target audience reached.

TEAR SHEET: A torn out page from a publication with an advertiser's ad, which is sent to the advertiser or their agency to verify publication.

TEASER CAMPAIGN: Ads that are not generally signed and are sometimes not clear as to what the subject is. Often they are a series of small-space advertisements. The intent is to generate interest and curiosity.

TEST CAMPAIGN: Testing an advertising idea in a narrow, local market before going to a broader audience. Essentially putting your big toe in the water before going all the way.

THUMBNAILS: Miniature, rough layouts, usually a couple of inches high and usually made with a pencil or Pentel, that depict the general positioning of elements and central idea of a TV or print advertisment or of a printed piece.

TOTAL AUDIENCE: The number of individual viewers tuned to a program for at least six minutes.

TPR: A time period rating—a general rating for a particular time period without considering what specific program is being broadcast. For example, the TPR for 8:00 P.M. is universally much higher than for 4:00 A.M.

TRAFFIC FLOW MAP: A geographic measure of pedestrian and vehicle densities, which is used to help determine which outdoor locations to purchase.

TRANSPARENCY: A color film through which light can pass as it does through a negative, but giving a positive image.

TRIM SIZE: The measurement of a magazine page after it has been trimmed in putting together the magazine. A little extra space in the mechanical is allowed for because of this trimming.

TYPOGRAPHY: The style, shapes, and sizes of the words as printed. The most important things to know as regards the creative character and feel of the piece you are working on are the two general classes of type: *serif*, of which the common *Times Roman* is a classic example, with its swirls and thick and thin lines, and *sans serif*, of which *Futura*, with its uniform-width lines and block letters, is a prime example.

UNAIDED RECALL: A test of which brand names are uppermost in a respondent's mind. For example, a typical unaided recall question might ask, "Consider the product category dandruff shampoo— which brand names do you immediately think of?"

VELOX: This is a photographic print that has been reproduced with halftone dots. Such reproduction allows the art to be shot as line art. Usually this is done to improve newspaper reproduction.

VERTICAL CUME: A measure of the total audience reached in two or more programs broadcast on the same day.

VERTICAL PUBLICATION: A magazine or paper that covers a specific industry or trade group.

VERTICAL SATURATION: Reaching as many people as possible in as short a time period as possible, by scheduling a great many commercials throughout the day for one or several days.

VIGNETTE: A photograph or illustration with an edge that is faded gradually into the background so that there is no hard line of separation.

WASTE CIRCULATION: This can mean that part of the circulation of a publication is in a geographic area where an advertised product is not distributed. It also can refer to those readers who are not potential customers for a featured product or service, such as the male portion of an audience exposed to a lipstick ad.

WEIGHT: An indication of the thickness of the paper to be used for a brochure or other printed piece. For example, in a given job, text paper might be 65 pounds and cover stock might be 100 pounds. This means that five hundred sheets of the text paper in a stated size would weigh 65 pounds, and five hundred sheets of the cover stock would weigh 100 pounds.

Index

Photo by Nancy Morse Conarroe.

Bob Fearon, formerly the International Promotion Director of *Time* magazine, the Corporate Advertising Director of IBM, and in recent years, the creative director of several advertising agencies, is today the President of The Creative Zone (TCZ Inc.), a New York city marketing communications firm which he describes as being "fanatically and ferociously focussed on provoking Eurekas."

He has indulged the educator in himself through his related professional activities which include having served on the Board of the Ad Council (for public service advertising), having been Executive Director of New York's Copy Club (The One Club), having written well over a hundred articles on advertising and the talented people who produce it, and now, of course, having authored this book. At the same time the eternal student in him is indulged through his continuing ties to The Hill School and Brown University (where he serves as a Trustee Emeritus).